"Tim Morey is a missionary to *our* culture. In *Embodying Our Faith* he demonstrates a robust commitment to sound biblical principles, practically applied, as the church produces disciples of Christ in a postmodern context. Illustrated with stories from a true pastor's heart, this book is one of the best examples I have seen of contextualization—applying the changeless truth of the gospel to the deep spiritual needs of a changing culture."

Dr. John Hutchison, professor of Bible exposition, Talbot School of Theology, Biola University, and founding member of Life Covenant Church

"How can the church stay both biblical and relevant for a postmodern generation that is mostly unreached, unchurched or dechurched? Tim Morey answers that question not from the ivory towers of academia (though he has certainly done his homework there!), but through a real-life ministry that is relational, missional and incarnational. This book should be read by anyone who longs to see the church thrive in the twenty-first century."

Mark L. Strauss, professor of New Testament, Bethel Seminary–San Diego

"Authority in our postmodern culture has been transferred from those people who merely talk about things in academic vacuums to those people who express their ideas in action and cultural engagement. Tim Morey is a leader who not only writes about how the church can witness to the gospel in this culture but demonstrates, through his own experience and the experience of his church, how we can enact it in a relevant, authentic and very biblical way. He is the sort of leader that I give authority to, and the picture of the church he paints and embodies is the sort of church I want to be a part of."

Adam S. McHugh, author of *Introverts in the Church*

Embodying Our Faith

Becoming a Living, Sharing,

Practicing Church

T i m   M o r e y

Foreword by Eddie Gibbs

IVP Books

An imprint of InterVarsity Press
Downers Grove, Illinois

InterVarsity Press
P.O. Box 1400, Downers Grove, IL 60515-1426
World Wide Web: www.ivpress.com
E-mail: email@ivpress.com

InterVarsity Press® is the book-publishing division of InterVarsity Christian Fellowship/USA®, a
movement of students and faculty active on campus at hundreds of universities, colleges and schools
of nursing in the United States of America, and a member movement of the International Fellowship
of Evangelical Students. For information about local and regional activities, write Public Relations
Dept., InterVarsity Christian Fellowship/USA, 6400 Schroeder Rd., P.O. Box 7895, Madison, WI
53707-7895, or visit the IVCF website at <www.intervarsity.org>.

Design: Cindy Kiple
Images: red hibiscus on background: Gonzalo Medina/iStockphoto
        white country church: Doug Landreth/Corbis

ISBN 978-0-8308-3729-8

Printed in the United States of America ∞

Library of Congress Cataloging-in-Publication Data

Morey, Tim, 1972-
  Embodying the faith: becoming a living, sharing, practicing church
  / Tim Morey.
      p. cm.
  Includes bibliographical references.
  ISBN 978-0-8308-3729-8 (pbk.: alk. paper)
  1. Church. 2. Discipling (Christianity) I. Title.
  BV600.3.M67 2009
  254'.5—dc22
                                                                        2009032079

| P | 18 | 17 | 16 | 15 | 14 | 13 | 12 | 11 | 10 | 9 | 8 | 7 | 6 | 5 | 4 | 3 | 2 | 1 |
| Y | 24 | 23 | 22 | 21 | 20 | 19 | 18 | 17 | 16 | 15 | 14 | 13 | 12 | 11 | 10 | 09 |

To my parents, Bob and Laura Morey,
who all my life have shown me
what it means to embody the faith.

Contents

Foreword

A younger generation of evangelicals have been walking away from established congregations out of disillusionment and frustration. I frequently heard comments in response such as "These angry young people are more certain of what they are against than what they are for." In contrast is Tim Morey, a young evangelical who is neither angry nor negative. Rather, he states his convictions with humility, grace and an evident love for the church not only within his own tradition but across the ecclesial spectrum.

Tim represents a growing number of church planters who have not "thrown the baby out with the bathwater." They retain the treasure of their spiritual inheritance while discarding some baggage. Tim works within the Evangelical Covenant denomination, which is strongly committed to church planting among the growing dechurched and never-churched segments of the population. This includes reaching out to immigrant groups to establish multiethnic, urban congregations and, as in the case of Tim, a commitment to reach out to those under age thirty-five. This age group is underrepresented in the churches of North America, whose numbers, as a churchgoing demographic, are shrinking the fastest.

As a missional leader in a rapidly changing cultural context, Tim recognizes the need for lifelong learning as the United States moves beyond the cultural paradigm of Christendom. Drawing on a wide body of literature, *Embodying Our Faith* identifies the foundational values and vision of Tim's church—Life Covenant in Torrance, California—and describes how these are being lived out in this emerging church. The book represents a reworking of his dissertation for the Fuller Seminary Doctor of Ministry program. I was privileged to have Tim in class, where we tried to imagine what missional churches in Western post-Christendom contexts might look like. Evangelicalism has tended to be stronger in critiquing culture than in engaging and creating it. The following pages represent a commendable example of applied missiology, a realization that, until the consummation of Christ's kingdom on his return to earth, every church is "emerging."

Tim is a discerning observer and interpreter of contemporary culture. More than that, he is leading his church to engage culture, seeking transformation. If the church is to impact our society today, it must recognize that it no longer enjoys a "home court advantage" but must gain a hearing among a cacophony of conflicting messages. If the church is to gain a hearing, it must be able to demonstrate convincingly the impact of its message, as well as declare its content with accuracy and clarity. A postmodern generation will judge the truth of a message by whether or not it is seen to be working.

The book's title, *Embodying Our Faith*, is well chosen. Tim addresses the challenge of turning undiscipled church members into authentic followers of Christ. He recognizes that the "about-turn" of conversion must be made with the intention of embarking on a life-long journey in company with fellow travelers in the steps of Jesus. Discipleship is not a second-stage, elitist concept; it is synonymous with being a Christian. Tim also stresses the importance of relationships that entail mutual accountability and ministry, encouragement and missional engagement. I pray that this work in progress, which will remain so throughout Tim's lifetime, will challenge his readers to join him on his journey.

Eddie Gibbs
Senior Professor
School of Intercultural Studies, Fuller Seminary

Preface

As a pastor in my thirties I get a lot of questions about the emerging generations and why they are not in the church. The absence of its children is becoming more and more pronounced as the church in the United States ages. More churches are realizing, contrary to their hopes, that the bulk of the younger generation will not begin attending once they grow up and have children.

I was in college when I returned to the church and committed myself to following Jesus. At that time I was deeply struck by the cultural distance that existed between the church and my generation. I was attending a contemporary church, but it still required a cultural leap to connect with much of what was happening there. I was spiritually hungry enough to make that leap but found that most of my peers were unwilling to give serious consideration to something that seemed so irrelevant and detached from their world. Since that time I have come to see this not just as a question of the preferences of a given body of worshipers but as deeply related to the apologetic we present.

I'm not the first (by a long shot) to bring up embodied apologetics. In fact the first time I can remember hearing the term was ten years ago when I read *Generating Hope* by Jimmy Long. But I haven't encountered books that unpack what an embodied apologetic might look like, or how we might intentionally structure church ministries to make an embodied apologetic part of the fabric of congregational life.

The apologetic I propose in *Embodying Our Faith* is experiential, communal and enacted. These dimensions correspond to the longings postmoderns have for transcendence, community and purpose. The church, as God's missionary people, must see its apologetic as part of a broader discussion that includes the need for critical contextualization and an understanding of Jesus' command that we be and make disciples. An embodied apologetic will be effective only when it is part of the everyday lives of church members, and as such we must make sure that those activities we declare normative in our churches serve our embodiment of the gospel.

I've read plenty, and I bet you have too, critiquing the church and scolding it for failing to live in the way of Jesus. I don't want to add to the criticism but rather to point one possible way forward. Today a lot of authors are discounting or abandoning the local church. On a pragmatic level there are days where I'm tempted to join them! But when I step back from the inevitable pain and disappointments that come from living out the faith among real people with all their flaws and messiness (who are gracious enough to accept me in my flaws and messiness), and especially as I revisit the words of Scripture, I am deeply convinced that the church is not an accident or tangential to the message and mission of Jesus. On the contrary, Jesus came to establish a people who would live as his followers and carry out his work until he returns. How blessed we are to be that people—to be his body, to be his bride.

I use my own church as an example not because I think we are perfect (far from it) but because this is the lab God has given me to live out my discipleship to Jesus and to do my best to lead others to do the same. The following pages are offered in humility because I know that while there are aspects of what I prescribe that our congregation is living beautifully, we still have a long way to go.

Our church is but one example among many. Many have wondered what the new model will be for churches in the coming generation (in the way Willow Creek and Saddleback were the model for many baby boomer churches). I do not believe there will be *one* model. Rather, the new model will be to create one's own model, to live as highly inquisitive missionaries who exegete the culture, understand both the believers and nonbelievers living in it, and build the church to function effectively in that context. There will be tremendous variety in the shapes that young missional churches take. This book examines one particular ministry context, with the hope that it will serve as an example of contextualization for others as well.

I have obtained permission from those involved to share almost all of the stories recounted in this book. Where it was inappropriate to do so, I have obscured details to let people remain anonymous.

I have a small army of people to thank, and even at that I won't be able to name everyone who has contributed to the thoughts contained in this book. First, I want to give a hearty thanks to everyone at Life Covenant Church. Thank you for allowing me the privilege of journeying with and leading you as we apprentice ourselves to Jesus and seek to live out his love for the world. May God bless us with a lifetime of walking together and seeing God do more than we could ask or imagine! Special thanks go to the outstanding men and women who lead Life, and in particular our vision team members past and present: Justin Robinson, Alex Viana, John Hutchison, Peter Thorrington, Chris Patay, Will Funk, Joel Hamilton, Brian Crowley and our first two planters, Doug Lee and Jon MacDonald. I could never overthank Life's associate pastor, my good friend Scott Buetzow, or overstate the blessing you are to me. Your influence on Life and on me is profound.

From my earliest days of ministry God has blessed me with a truly amazing succession of mentors: James Dalbey, Chuck Price, Bill MacPhee, Craig McConnell, John Hutchison, Wayne Carlson, Charlie Barker and Dave Olson. Thank you for considering speaking into my life part of your ministry. My professors at Fuller had tremendous influence on this book and on our church: Eddie Gibbs, Dallas Willard, Keith Matthews, Brian McLaren and Terry Walling. Thank you for investing in the next generation of leaders. And many thanks go to Tom Sine, who was kind enough to recommend this project to IVP.

My editor, Dave Zimmerman, was incredibly helpful in taking what began as a doctoral dissertation and adapting it in such a way that it would not cause instant sleep in those who choose to pick it up (at least we hope this is the case; if you fall asleep, I still accept the blame). Three unofficial editors pored over this manuscript as well, and greatly strengthened it in the process: my friends Dan Palomino, Justin Robinson and David Beck. I hope that in the finished product my thoughts are cogent and winsome enough that you, the reader, might actually enjoy this book, find it a blessing to your ministry, and perhaps even worthy of recommending to a friend.

Finally, my deepest thanks go to my family. This book is dedicated to my parents, who throughout my life have lived humbly and simply as great examples of real faith lived out in ordinary, everyday life. My wonderful wife has been so supportive and encouraging through this whole process. Samantha, if you didn't believe in me like you do I don't know if I would have the courage to put my thoughts in print. And my beautiful daughters so motivate me. I pray that Abby and Hannah grow up in a church where becoming like Jesus and living as kingdom missionaries is as natural as breathing.

My prayer is that God will use my words, humbly and fearfully offered, to help us live more authentically as apprentices of Jesus, deeply loved by the Father, and sent by and with him into the world. To God be the glory.

Tim Morey
Matthew 6:33

Introduction

Unreached, Unchurched
and Dechurched

*I must proclaim the good news of the kingdom of God to the
other towns also, because that is why I was sent.*

LUKE 4:43

*The way forward for the Christian faith will be for evangelical Christians
to stop shrugging or twitching at the mention of postmodernism,
and get on with engaging the culture with God's timeless
message in a critical and thoughtful manner.*

GRAHAM JOHNSTON,
PREACHING TO A POSTMODERN WORLD

One of the scariest days of my life was the day we started Life
Covenant Church. I don't think I realized how stressed I actually
was until I found myself in the back room of our house (a.k.a. the
church office) wiping sweat from my forehead and trying not to
swear out loud at my new printer/copier/fax machine for refusing
to give me my notes. It was ten minutes past our start time, people
were milling about in our living room (a.k.a. the sanctuary), and I
felt all at once like crying, throwing up and pounding my new
printer with a hammer.

Bundled in among my fears ("*What if no one comes? Or if they don't come back? What if I can't support my family? Is Starbucks hiring? What does it say about me if I fail?*") was one question that was less directly tied to my ego but pressed on me all the same: would we be a church that actually made a difference or just another bunch of religious consumers? The idea driving us, after all, was not to gather a crowd to hear my wonderful teachings or to create a venue with hipper music than the place down the street—it was to live as a community of people on mission, helping one another become more like Jesus and carrying out his work in the world. It was these things, not the presence of splashy programs or clever ways to attract people, that defined for us what it meant to be a missional church. So, if God blessed us with the privilege of making an impact, would we be faithful to step into that opportunity? Or would we end up as a roomful of pew potatoes, our presence on Sundays masking the spiritual lethargy that characterized our daily lives?

In his provocative book *The Great Giveaway*, David Fitch poses a powerful question, couched in a parable of sorts. Imagine a new church that grows rapidly from a handful of committed individuals to a Sunday attendance of one thousand people. Yet, in spite of the number of people present on Sundays, only one hundred people are truly known to one another, serve, give, actively pursue a life of becoming like Christ and living out his mission in the world. Fitch asks, Is this a church of one thousand or a church of one hundred?[1] To put it a different way, if we aren't living like a church, are we a church? If we don't care about being transformed into the image of Christ or about the world God loves, can we call ourselves a church? Is a church a church if it exists only for itself?

There was a time when having a crowd would have been enough for me. Whether that crowd was being spiritually formed to look like Jesus, or whether God's mission in the world was truly embraced and lived out would have been secondary, at best. I wanted to succeed, which for me mostly meant lots of people. I don't think it's a coincidence that several years passed between the time God put church planting in my heart and the time when he opened the door for me to actually do it. I wasn't ready (on more levels than I realized), and God in his mercy gave me more time on the bench than I wanted (I have many days when I wonder if I still need more).

Mixed motives notwithstanding, my desire to be a church planter came out of my desire to see my generation meet Jesus. I was born into a strong Christian home and received Christ at the ripe old age of five. I saw a lot growing up in the church, much of which was beautiful, some of which was not. My family was part of a number of churches ranging from very conservative Baptist to very charismatic. Along the way there was Calvary Chapel, the house church movement, a little bit of United Methodist, more Baptist. I can remember wonderful, godly people in all of them, but also a lot of wreckage. We were part of two churches that split, two which saw fights over color-of-the-carpet issues escalate to the point where good-hearted pastors were run out of the church, one where a pastor's affair caused the church to implode overnight. By the time I left the church in my teens, I had become disillusioned, confused, angry. I had lost faith in the church and was eager to leave it behind. My detour from the church lasted about five years, during which time I immersed myself in a stew of hedonism on the one hand, and a search for any philosophy or worldview that might allow me to settle into a comfortable, guilt-free agnosticism on the other.

I was midway through college when the love of Jesus recaptured me. I truly felt reborn and was anxious for my friends to experience what I was experiencing. This wasn't easy. I didn't have the verbiage for it at the time, but what I quickly found was that my church, which was a truly wonderful place, was not a good cultural fit for me and my peers. The church prided itself in being contemporary. It had a genuine love for the lost, and its staff attended ministry conferences at Saddleback and Willow Creek. But for me, to say nothing of my unsaved peers, it felt foreign, out of place. It wasn't just the programs or the style of music; it was the posture, the place the church seemed to occupy in the world. So much about the church felt foreign, as if it had been plucked out of another time or place. It was hard to picture the church as a place you would go if you were really looking to find answers about life, God and reality.

I understood, even then, that people would stumble over the cross. But it felt like I had to get them past an array of stumbling blocks just to get to the one stumbling block that mattered. And so as I began to feel God's pull toward vocational ministry, a question began to brew in me: Is there a way that we as the church can be faithfully, even radically, biblical, and at the same time be culturally relevant? This question has led me into deep love for and deep frustration with the church, through nine years serving in two church-based college ministries in Southern California and, since 2003, as a church planter leading a young church in Torrance, California.

MINISTERING FROM THE MARGINS

Torrance, like most of Southern California, is very unchurched (plausible estimates put the unchurched population at about 95 percent).[2] So when we launched Life, we were under no illusions that this was going to be easy. One pastor friend told me, "Good luck. Torrance is where church plants go to die."

Sometimes I hear stories from older pastors of days gone by and it seems like they are talking about churches that existed in a whole different country, or at least in a radically different culture. A steady flow of conversions, young singles and families streaming through their doors, building programs to accommodate all the growth. Many of these pastors tell their stories with a sense of nostalgia, for they too realize they are speaking of a different time, even if the place is the same. The culture has shifted under our feet and ministry looks increasingly different.

For a long time the church in the United States has enjoyed a sort of home-court advantage. The nation was culturally Christian, and the language that we used to describe God, salvation, heaven, hell, Scripture and other religious concepts was understood by the vast majority of Americans. When we spoke about God or Jesus, we could reasonably assume that roughly the same image would come to mind for the listener. The average person held values that were marginally Judeo-Christian, had never met a Buddhist or a Muslim, and didn't question whether truth existed or could be known.

All this is changing. As our culture moves deeper into the twenty-first century, none of these assumptions holds true. The term *God* will likely bring to mind any number of images, from a theistic God as in Christianity, Islam or Judaism, to a deistic god who had something to do with creation but is now uninvolved in the world, to god as an impersonal force as in Buddhist and New Age teachings, or god as one of a pantheon of spiritual beings as in Hindu teachings. Perhaps most likely of all, mentioning God will invoke the squishy, nondescript god of pluralism; the god who can be reached no matter what we think he or she might be like, and who accepts pilgrims who have taken any religious path to reach the deity. This god (if personal) is inevitably loving, approves of (or is at least indifferent to) various lifestyles and in the unlikely event that he or she will judge people for their actions, judgment will only fall on those more wicked than you or I. The God of Abraham, Isaac and Jacob has given way to the god of Oprah, Eckhart Tolle and *The Secret.* America might be best described as post-Christian, and tenets of postmodern thinking which once were fringe have trickled into our culture and become normal.

UNREACHED, UNCHURCHED AND DECHURCHED

In 2007 the Barna Group released an important study on attitudes toward Christians held by sixteen- to twenty-nine-year-olds in the United States. Their top three impressions were that Christians are antihomosexual (an opinion held by 91 percent of young outsiders), judgmental (87 percent) and hypocritical (85 percent).[3]

In our context these observations ring true as we listen to our friends outside the church. In looking at the religious landscape of the emerging generations, there are three terms our church finds helpful in describing those who are outsiders to the church: *unreached*, *unchurched* and *dechurched*.

First, the *unreached* are those who, for all intents and purposes, know nothing about the Christian faith or the gospel message. Many find it surprising that so many members of the younger generations have never heard the message or at least have never understood it well enough to accept or reject it for what it is. For many, their understanding of Christianity is pieced together from observing a combination of televangelists, political activists and the Christian spokespersons who show up on television news programs. Many others, though, have some personal experience with Christians, and this only adds to their bad impression of the church.[4] Though they live in a culture where many Christians also live, they are still best thought of as essentially unreached.

George Barna and others have defined an *unchurched* person as someone who has not attended a church service (other than a wedding or a funeral) in at least six months. This term has been widely applied to the baby boomer generation but also fits well with the emerging generations. The primary difference is that the younger generations have far less familiarity with the church than do their parents' generation. This changes the flavor of what it looks like to be unchurched. Baby boomers frequently have been portrayed as rebelling against a church they had grown up in, while the younger generations typically have not grown up in the church.[5] Tom

Beaudoin writes, "Many baby boomers had kept institutional religion at arm's length until midlife. For their children, GenXers, the step from religion-as-accessory to religion-as-unnecessary was a slight shuffle, not a long leap."[6]

Our church uses the term *dechurched* for those who once were involved in the church but have become disillusioned and left (a population that God seems especially pleased to bring to our church). Dissatisfaction with the church runs high with the younger generations, and many report experiencing the church as hypocritical, judgmental, boring or irrelevant, or have had bad experiences with church members or church leadership. According to David Kinnaman's research, the majority of young adults outside the church fall into this category.[7] Some of these formerly churched individuals never had genuine faith in Christ, while others have retained their faith in Christ but lost faith in the church, and still others have lost faith in both. In any case, the typical dechurched person approaches the church with the caution of one who has been burned and expects to be burned again.

It is sobering to look at the number of people who fall into these categories. Church allegiance in America is in serious decline, even as interest in spirituality is on the rise. Pollsters tell us that Americans are more spiritual now than at any time in the past fifty years.[8] At the same time, people are increasingly trading in a stated allegiance to a particular religion for a "none of the above" (or perhaps a hodgepodge of the above) approach to the spiritual.[9] Between 1990 and 2001 the number of Americans who said they have no religion doubled to more than 29.4 million (which is more than the combined number of Methodists, Lutherans and Episcopalians in the United States).[10] To those who pay attention to the fiction and nonfiction books on the bestseller list and the films and television programs that deal with spiritual topics, this might not come as much of a surprise.

Another very important study in 2008 deals with the actual

numbers of people attending church.[11] Statistics on U.S. church attendance are increasingly recognized as sorely inflated. To the bewilderment of pastors around the country, both Barna and Gallup report that 40 to 47 percent of American adults attend church on a typical weekend, yet these numbers are based on respondents' self-reporting. In what is termed the *halo effect*, it seems that respondents frequently report that they attend church far more often than they actually do (similar inflations occur when responding to questions about voting and sex).[12] When numbers based on actual head counts (as opposed to respondents' self-reporting) are used, the percentage of attending adults drops to a more believable 17.5 percent (combined evangelical, mainline, Catholic and Orthodox churches as of 2005).[13] What's more, this number is steadily declining, even as the U.S. population grows. The church is not keeping up.

Beyond this, approximately 3,700 churches close their doors permanently every year (71 per week). New churches are being started as well, but not nearly fast enough. In order to keep up with population growth, nearly 7,000 new churches would be needed each year (or 2,900 more than are currently started each year).[14] If these trends continue, David T. Olson predicts that church attendance will drop to 14.7 percent by 2020.[15] Projections like these, coupled with the far more radical decline in Europe and the amazing growth of Christianity in Latin America, Africa and Asia, have led Professor Philip Jenkins to quip that, by midcentury, the phrase "a white Christian" will sound like an oxymoron, as odd and surprising as hearing about "a Swedish Buddhist."[16]

The situation is even more serious when considering young people in the United States. Indeed, a large portion of the decline seen in these numbers is the result of the postmodern generation's nonparticipation in the church. Back in 1998 the World Values Society reported that only 12 percent of the thirty-one million young people in the United States go to church, and 88 percent of those who attended as teens dropped out of the church by their sophomore year of college (a figure that, as a former college pastor, I find entirely believable).[17] Some in established churches would characterize this nonparticipation as youthful rebellion. However, as Leonard Sweet points out, *rebellion* presupposes some level of intimacy with what they are rebelling against. On the whole, this is not the case with this generation, as fewer of them have been raised in the familiarity of the traditions and rituals of the church, and, even among those who have, there has been an ever-widening disconnect between the church and the world they live in.[18]

This unfamiliarity is evidenced in the low numbers of young adults who identify themselves as Christians, and the even lower numbers of those whose responses to questions about Jesus, salvation, heaven and the like who indicate that they have any kind of personal relationship with Christ. According to researcher Thom Rainer of Southern Baptist Seminary, extensive interviewing of Americans in different generational groups indicates that 15 percent of Gen Xers and only 4 percent of generation Y (age seventeen and older) are likely born-again Christians.[19]

This seems to be confirmed anecdotally by those in parachurch organizations and elsewhere who have witnessed the decreasing effectiveness of traditional evangelism methods with the emerging generations. Noteworthy too is the observation that Eddie Gibbs and Ryan Bolger make that while there are some large emerging churches, most are thirty to one hundred people.[20] On the one hand this reflects a preference many younger evangelicals have for smaller communities of faith, yet I believe it is a reflection of the difficulty of evangelism with this population as well.

Reggie McNeal points to another sobering trend among young Christians. Many of those leaving the church are doing so not because they have lost their faith but to preserve their faith. Their contention is that the church no longer contributes to their faith, but instead has become a detriment to it.[21] This observation rings eerily true from my own experience in ministering to the emerging generations, and also coincides with Mike Regele's research that Gen Xers are almost 60 percent more likely to report leaving the church due to disillusionment (to become dechurched) than are older generations.[22]

THE CHURCH RESPONDS

The response of many churches to the absence of the postmodern generation is denial. Many have downplayed the cultural changes that have occurred, while others have consciously written off any attempt at reaching postmoderns and hope or assume that they will return when they have children themselves or otherwise "grow up" (an ironic statement when you consider that older Xers are approaching their forties). These churches see little need for change on their part and instead wait for their prodigal children to return, and for those who were never part of the church in the first place to come to them.

Other churches see the need to be proactive and are responding by launching alternative worship services they hope will capture the allegiance of this generation. This response has met with some success in places, but churches find that meaningful assimilation into the larger church body is often quite difficult. Some of these churches undertake this approach with the unstated assumption that once these young people mature a bit, they will abandon the alternative service and start attending the "real" church service. For these, little is accomplished long term. The problem faced in trying to get their graduating high school students to join the adults has only been postponed.

Noble as this approach may be, in settings where the implications of having two distinct congregations in one have not been well-anticipated, tensions between the alternative and traditional worship services commonly rise to the point where the alternative service is shut down or pushed out. Success stories in this arena are few and far between, but for many churches this still is the most viable option. (I was once very close to starting one of these services, and attended a how-to conference with my senior pastor. The event looked like a father-son convention. Fifty-somethings with graying temples and blue blazers were accompanied by twenty- and thirty-somethings sporting jeans and goatees. Emerging church pioneer Dieter Zander stood before us and sounded a cautionary note: "I've planted a church and I've started an alternative service within a church, and the second is about 50 percent harder than starting a church from scratch.")

Another approach is seen more and more, which I think is both realistic and honorable. Some churches, looking at the reality of the situation, see the need for change in bringing the gospel to this culture, but must honestly admit that, for whatever reasons, they are not capable of making the needed changes. Instead, they choose to serve as parents or grandparents, using their financial resources and wisdom to empower others to reach those they cannot. Life Covenant Church is the recipient of this kind of blessing. Much of our start-up cost was covered by a hundred-year-old church in a small farming town three hundred miles from Torrance. They sensed a tremendous burden to see the younger generations reached, and the way they expressed this was by participating in the launch of a church which had taken on that mission.

In addition to this, a number of adults in their fifties and sixties joined Life specifically to serve as "missionaries." In some ways I had the worst sales pitch ever, and looking back I can't believe some said yes. My spiel went something like:

> We are part of an underparented generation that desperately needs mentors. We need you, but this isn't going to be about you. I need people who love this generation so much that

they'll lay aside their preferences and be there for them in the midst of their messy lives. You're going to ask if we can do such and such the way you used to, and I'm going to say no. You're going to ask me to turn down the music, and I'm going to say no. But we need you, and I hope God is calling you to be part of this.

A handful of people said yes, and I can't imagine Life existing without these dedicated servants. Their contribution to the church in wisdom, mentoring relationships, leadership and finances has been greater than what anyone could calculate. And to my delight, they love the church! Yesterday I was with our leaders on a weekend retreat, and one of these pillars of the church looked at the rest of us with tears in his eyes and said, "I've grown more in these last few years with you than I ever did in my past church experiences."

This last approach seems to resonate especially well with church planters, as most church plants start with an intuitive understanding that they will not be able to reach everyone in a given community. (While many established churches have this understanding too, I am surprised how often I encounter churches that truly believe they are a church that will appeal to everyone.) Especially in diverse areas it is understood that it will take a family of churches to reach all the different types of people. For those churches who already see themselves starting other churches that will be more effective at reaching certain groups, such an approach to reaching the younger generations makes sense.[23]

All of these approaches, however, run the danger of missing the point. Many (if not most) churches hold an underlying assumption that if only they "did church" better, people would come. While our churches will always have room for improvement, this is not the real issue. As Reggie McNeal points out, the culture around us does not wake up each day thinking they would go to church if only there were a good one to attend.

> Church leaders seem unable to grasp this simple implication
> of the new world—people outside the church think church is
> for church people, not for them. We may have saturated the
> market of people who want to be part of the church culture,
> who want church the way we do it in North America.[24]

In response to this reality we must become missionaries to our
culture. Rather than pretending no changes are needed or attempting cosmetic fixes, we need to apply ourselves to the hard work of
understanding the culture God has placed us in, while prayerfully
bringing the gospel to that place in a language and manner understandable to those we seek to reach. This task of living as missionaries is multifaceted, and a necessary component is understanding
how postmodernism has shaped the worldview of the emerging
generations.

POSTMODERNISM AT STARBUCKS

In the last decade legions of books have been written on postmodernism, and many have been helpful in my attempts to understand
the surrounding culture. At the same time most of the people we
interact with are not philosophy students. They neither know nor
care about postmodernism as a philosophy, yet they are influenced
by it all the same. Much of this worldview has seeped into the
popular mindset, and I think in many ways it is more helpful to
talk about postmodernism as a cultural phenomenon with certain
characteristics than it is to talk about it as a philosophy. In the
remainder of this chapter I hope to distill a few of the major implications of this shift as they trickle down to the level of the average
latte-sipper at Starbucks.

The Western world is in the midst of a titanic cultural shift. The
worldview known as modernism, which has been firmly in place
for several centuries, is being shaken from its once-firm position

and replaced by a new worldview. This emerging worldview is postmodernism, and the era we live in is called postmodernity. More than anything, this shift is a revolution in how people think; how they understand, take in and process information.[25]

The modern era relied heavily upon human reason, the reliability of science, the inevitability and goodness of human progress and technology, and placed great value on individualism.[26] However, the late twentieth century has seen the foundations of modernism crumble.

Sociologists attribute the demise of modernism to a number of factors, including communication and technological advances such as the invention of the microchip, the rise of the personal computer, the dominance of television and the proliferation of the Internet. In addition, historical events such as the assassinations of John F. Kennedy and Martin Luther King Jr., the cultural and sexual revolutions, the fall of the Berlin Wall, the Columbine massacre, and 9/11 have served to undermine the tenets of modernism. Setting the stage for this breakdown is the failure of modernity to deliver what it promised. At its peak in the mid-twentieth century, modernity had failed to scientifically explain life's origins or cure cancer (or even the common cold), let alone explain spiritual realities. Similarly, the modern belief that technology would lead to a better world has faltered in a century that has seen war, human misery, treachery and pollution increase, seemingly without limits. These factors, combined with the globalization of knowledge via the Internet, have led to a collapse in the modern worldview and the subsequent rise of postmodernism.[27]

This is not to say that modernity is completely dead—far from it. Much of the world is in fact still functionally premodern, with a highly spiritual, prescientific view of the world; and people who immigrate to the United States bring much of this worldview with them. In addition to being prepared to minister to postmodern people, the Christian leader of today will need to be able to minister to those with modern and premodern worldviews as well.[28]

Some understanding of postmodernism is important for any-one reaching out to the culture, but it is especially important in reaching the younger generations. Although postmodernism is not age specific and has a significant impact on all of us, it most dramatically affects the younger generations—this is the domi-nant worldview into which we were born. Consequently, we have little knowledge of anything different, and postmodern thinking has become a part of the value system that comes naturally. Fish are the last to discover the water, and the postmodern generations are largely unaware of the "water" they swim in. Three broad, in-terrelated categories will help us distill the way postmodern thought has shaped the thinking of the culture around us.

Deconstruction.

First speaker: *"Here's the answer. That's the way it is."*
Second speaker: *"I doubt it."*
Welcome to postmodernity.[29]

Postmodernism is virtually synonymous with radical doubt and skepticism. The philosophical framework standing behind this is known as deconstruction. Deconstruction concerns the use of language, the realities (or lack thereof) that words represent and the power inherent in words and those who wield them. De-constructionists assert that language does not describe reality but constructs it. Therefore, we must deconstruct the language people use and the truth claims that they make to determine the pur-poses for which their claims are being used.[30] In its most radical forms, deconstruction asserts that there is no truth, only interpre-tation.[31] In its less radical forms, deconstruction tells us that a gap exists between our words and the realities they seek to describe, and that certainty of knowledge is an impossibility.[32]

Under deconstruction, all previous assumptions are challenged and taken apart whenever possible. Within this schema, historical "facts" are suspect, and science and reason as means of acquiring knowledge are rejected as either incomplete or altogether faulty.[33] The inherent good of human progress is also rejected. Metanarratives, stories that seek to transcend local cultures with an overarching story that applies to all cultures, are particularly troublesome to deconstructionists. All universal stories connecting different cultures are seen as oppressive and intolerant, attempts to impose one culture's norms on another.[34] The result is deep skepticism about truth, especially that espoused by powerful people or institutions. The opening scene of Mel Gibson's *Braveheart* captures the deconstructionist mood well: "History is written by those who have hanged heroes."

In practice, few outside of a university's philosophy or literature department hold to this theory (and an increasing number of philosophers assert that deconstruction is itself dying).[35] However, a good number of the assumptions made by deconstructionists have made their way into the popular imagination. When asked if something that is true for one person has to be true for another, the postmodern generation resoundingly answers no. The recognition of the power of words to distort and deceive has made emerging generations skeptical toward those in authority and institutions that exert control over others (such as the government, family and church). I believe Green Day's *American Idiot* became a huge hit in large part because it expresses well the perception (which once may have been considered paranoid but is now common) that those in power try to fool everyone else so their own power is not threatened.

Adding to this distrust, the postmodern generations' coming of age took place at a time when divorce rates were skyrocketing and hyper-individualism and the pursuit of wealth caused deep fragmentation in the family. The reigning experts used scientific research to bolster and affirm the decisions that Gen Xers' parents (and they themselves) were making, assuring society that latchkey kids would be okay and that single-parent homes were just as good as a traditional nuclear family. The result: a generation that has difficulty trusting others, is skeptical of claims to truth and displays a deep longing for community.

Moral relativism. In relativism the objectivity of knowledge and the absolute nature of truth are denied and replaced with an understanding that what can be known is severely restricted by the experiences and preconceptions of the knower. Truth is relative. It is at best unknowable and at worst is a mere construct that has no objective existence. Therefore, any claims to universal or absolute truths, morals or values are also rejected. Morality is seen as relative to the culture or tribe from which it comes. Truth is seen as personal and is generally determined by our own experience of what works for an individual or for a particular community. As Chuck Smith Jr. has said, "Gen X does not look for truth in religion, science, or philosophy but in personal experience, intuition, and assumption. Xers are skeptical of people who make claims to the truth and wonder what they are trying to sell."[36]

The average postmodern has little difficulty holding to statements, truth claims or moral stances that are in contradiction to one another. When pushed to logically reconcile contradictory views, the response may well be a shrugging "whatever." Since each person (or community) defines its own morality, sin is a nonissue for many in the emerging generations, and "That's true for you, but not for me" has become a mantra. Consequently, one of the greatest offenses we can commit in the postmodern world is to suggest that what is true or moral for me might also be true or moral for you. Postmodern sentiments are summed up in the words of Sheryl Crow, "If it makes you happy, it can't be that bad."

Religious pluralism. Pluralism is the application of deconstruction and relativism to the religious realm, and can be safely identified as the religion of choice among postmoderns. Religious pluralism is the belief that all religious systems are equally true. Many sum up this view in the Buddhist-Hindu statement that "many paths lead to the top of the mountain." In this system of thought, no religion can be judged superior to or "truer" than any other.[37]

Christianity has lost the cultural position of privilege it has enjoyed since Constantine. Religions are casually blended, and preference is given to inclusive and experiential Eastern religions. As a faith with very particular truth claims, Christianity is seen as synonymous with intolerance, exclusivism, condemnation, bigotry and oppression. John Stackhouse describes postmoderns as those who like their religion "à la carte." "I want a little Confucianism to organize my life, a little tai chi for strength and balance, a weekend tantric sex workshop for spice, and the twenty-third Psalm when I overdo things and get into trouble."[38]

A parable of our culture's approach to religion can be found in a common feature of our neighborhoods: the supermarket. We are accustomed to tremendous variety in our foods and the freedom to purchase our favorite brands. We would not settle for anyone telling us that his or her favorite brand is the only correct choice, so why would we do so with our religious beliefs and choices?[39] As a culture, "we are not moving towards a godless land but to a land with many gods."[40]

Under the influence of globalization, the United States has become a new mission frontier. The influx of new religious ideas and philosophies can be seen on the average university campus today in the variety of religious clubs offered to students. As well as Campus Crusade for Christ or InterVarsity Christian Fellowship, one can typically find clubs for Muslim, Jewish, Wiccan, Hindu, Baha'i, Buddhist or Satanist students. At one time Torrance's community college even boasted a club for religiously practicing vampires.

This variety (combined with relativism) has resulted in a salad bar approach where we are free to choose whatever faith (or parts of faiths) seem appealing, and to both alter that faith at will and express it in unique forms (like expressing it in and through pop culture).[41] It is important to recognize here that we are no longer talking about the somewhat familiar situation of people saying no to church but yes to Jesus. Whereas, even fifteen years ago, that may have commonly been the case, today "increasing numbers are looking for a transcendent spirituality in which Jesus no longer occupies a central place."[42]

Since the underlying assumption is that all paths lead to God, it is common for the postmodern to identify with several faiths at once. In creating their own customized religion, the choice comes back to one main determining factor: "What counts as religious must meet the ultimate test: Xers' own personal experience."[43]

CONCLUSION

The postmodern situation presents a number of challenges for the church. How do we bring the message of Jesus to a culture that is deeply skeptical about truth claims, rejects metanarratives (such as the gospel), considers the church a suspect institution, takes offense at moral judgments and believes any religion will lead them to God?

There is a sense in which this is familiar territory. In many ways our missionary situation is more like the world of the New Testament and the early centuries of the church than the subsequent eras. In his important book *The Mission of God*, Christopher J. H. Wright reminds us that Christianity has a long history of engaging "postmodern" challenges. From the beginning, Christ's church has lived in cultures with differing systems of morality, religious pluralism, syncretism and deep skepticism over the claims made by Christians.[44] Only in the West, and only in recent centuries, has the church ministered within a predominantly Christian culture.

While the challenges we face as Western Christians in the

twenty-first century are daunting, we should not lose heart. Even as these cultural shifts present new challenges, they present tremendous opportunities as well. Postmoderns hunger for meaning and purpose, feel the need for community and unbroken relationships, are open to spirituality and mystery, and desire to experience the real and genuine. We have the opportunity to lead people into a relationship with the real God of the universe, to provide caring communities where Christ's love is lived out, to offer a life with meaning and purpose, and to offer real hope for this life and the next.

I believe this is a great moment for the church. The church, now relegated to a marginalized role in society, has the opportunity to recover its vocation as God's missionary people. This situation will require churches to study the Scriptures and our culture, lean heavily on the Holy Spirit's guidance and power, and relearn how to think like missionaries. To that end, we will begin with an examination of our apologetic.

I

Show and Tell

Why We Need an Embodied Apologetic

Let your light shine before others, that they may see
your good deeds and glorify your Father in heaven.

MATTHEW 5:16

As we move into the emerging culture . . .
our apologetic will focus more and more on beauty, goodness,
experience, questions, mystery, community, and humility.

BRIAN McLAREN AND TONY CAMPOLO,
ADVENTURES IN MISSING THE POINT

"I don't believe in God anymore." The e-mail was from a former student in my college group. "That's the first time I've 'thought' that out loud, and I've been afraid to admit it, but I'd be lying to myself if I said otherwise." He went on to say that he kind of wanted it to be true, but then to list for several pages reasons why it probably was not. Some objections were intellectual, though many more were experiential, coming out of his own exposure to Christianity. "How," he asked in a dozen different ways, "can I possibly believe this is true?"

My friend represents that strange combination of longing and hesitancy that we see so often, and a blend of intellectual questions with questions of the heart. Christianity claims to be so good, but is this really as good as it gets? He knew all the answers Christians had for his questions, found nearly all of them logical, some even likely—but the answers had no weight. His skepticism stemmed in large part from his experience with the church, and his university experience just fanned the flames of his doubts. His skepticism was heavy—so much so that reasoned answers alone couldn't tip the scales to overcome his doubts. Even with logical answers firmly in hand, the gap between what the church says is true and the way it actually lives looms large. Rather than supporting the reasons for faith, the church's practice often weighs against its being true.

How do we bring truth to people who are so skeptical of truth? Millard Erickson asks and answers the question this way: "Can a deconstructed horse even be led to water? . . . *Yes, but you have to use a deconstructed rope*."[1] The gospel is the power of God unto salvation, and it can most certainly reach people in our post-Christian world. But the methods will have to fit who they are, while remaining faithful to Scripture. As with any missions endeavor, the gospel will have to be brought in a way that makes sense to the hearers. Leonard Sweet provocatively states, "I am a virtual fundamentalist about content. I am a virtual libertarian about containers."[2] The "containers" in which the church brings the gospel will look different for those brought up with a more postmodern worldview.

My position is that as we move deeper into a post-Christian twenty-first century, the people of God will need to rediscover the power of an embodied apologetic. By this I mean an apologetic that is based more on the weight of our actions than the strength of our arguments. This is an apologetic that is high-touch, engages people relationally, ordinarily takes place in the context of an ongoing friendship, and addresses the needs inquirers have and the questions they pose. It provides the weight to our answers that reason by itself cannot.

ADAPTING OUR APOLOGETICS

According to historical theologian Robert Webber, the early church incarnated its message in such a way that people recognized it as truth. Though appeals to reason were an important part of early church apologetics as well, they did not dominate evangelistic methods until much later in church history. Particularly as Enlightenment epistemology took hold and empirical methodology moved to center stage as the most trustworthy way to discern what is true, the church's apologetic properly followed and became more rational and evidence based.[3]

There is always a temptation for the church to stick with what is familiar and has worked in the past. The early church faced this when its mission spread beyond Jerusalem and Judea to the Samaritans and the Gentiles. In their case, the experience led to the church wrestling through both the content of the gospel message and the way it would be presented (Acts 15). At the Jerusalem council the church reached a conclusion that clarified the message of the gospel, insuring that their telling of the story was faithful ("We believe it is through the grace of our Lord Jesus that we are saved, just as they are" [Acts 15:11]), and that their presentation of this message was not obstructed by unnecessary cultural baggage ("We should not make it difficult for the Gentiles who are turning to God" [Acts 15:19]). The church, embracing its identity as the missionary people of God, took pains to see that the message would not be distorted, yet would be presented in a way that the Gentiles would be able to receive, understand and grow in the gospel as God matured them. At the same time, sensitivity was shown that the faith of the Gentiles would not be practiced in reckless ways that would hinder the progress of the gospel among the Jews living in Gentile lands (Acts 15:20-21, 29).

The church has faced this challenge at numerous cultural crossroads along the way as well. In the time of Augustine, encroaching paganism brought a serious challenge to the Christian story which society had accepted. The challenge was serious enough that many feared the collapse of the church. In response to this Augustine refashioned his telling of the Christian story (in *The City of God*) in such a way that it remained true to Scripture yet addressed the current challenges being raised by its opponents. Augustine's response in many ways shaped the apologetic the church successfully brought to pagan Europe for centuries to come.[4]

Similarly, Thomas Aquinas's *Summa Contra Gentiles* was a retelling of the gospel to address the challenge brought by the looming threat of Islam. Prior to this work the missionaries of Aquinas's day ignored Islam as long as possible, preferring instead to bring the message to the pagan cultures of Europe where their apologetic had already proved effective. To evangelize the Muslim world required a new approach with a new apologetic—one that corresponded to the thinking and worldview of this new mission field.

We face a similar challenge in our time. It seems in some ways as if our apologetic, which has largely been shaped as a response to modernism, has been perfected just as the rules of the game have changed. Modernism, with its idolization of reason, progress, individualism and scientific naturalism, was originally perceived as a tremendous threat to the gospel. The challenges presented by this worldview seemed daunting, and indeed, continue to be formidable. Yet, over time the church responded with a new, finely reasoned apologetic that was well-suited to the challenge of the day.

As the church's apologetic has become more nuanced and effective, the church has grown comfortable with the modern worldview as the primary challenger to the Christian worldview. The tools necessary to construct a modern apologetic (e.g., reason, evidence, scientific method) have arguably become so identified with evangelical Christianity that, to some, the suggestion of a different set of tools strikes the ears as something close to heresy. Erwin

McManus observes, "Where once modernity was seen as the enemy of the church, today it seems that Christian thinkers run to modernity's side to find protection from what is hidden in the shadows of the postmodern world."[5]

In the apologetics of modernism, we were best equipped to defend the faith against the atheist or perhaps the scientifically minded agnostic. In the postmodern context, however, the debate is rarely theism versus atheism, even though this is likely what seminary training prepared its pastors for.[6] More likely, the existence of God is presupposed, and the question we encounter is that of religious pluralism: does any one faith have the right to claim it has the truth? Proving God's existence "may well have been necessary in the modern era, but the existence of God is not as much of a question today. A bigger issue might be which God and why."[7] Describing the postmodern mission field, Curtis Chang says, "The challenger is not the aggressive secular humanist who attacks the rationality of Christianity, but [one] who holds to a personally constructed epistemology of radical doubt. The old arguments no longer hold sway."[8] Many churches (particularly those who are consciously attempting to engage postmodern people) are beginning to ask what kind of apologetic will be effective in this new context.

The Scriptures are rich with instruction in this matter, as the world of the first century paralleled ours in many ways. Spirituality was deeply embraced, nearly everyone held to some religious faith, and Christianity was seen as an odd choice on the religious menu. Conversion was largely an unnecessary inconvenience because a person could comfortably add more gods to his or her worship without these gods demanding exclusive allegiance. Like twenty-first-century believers, the early Christians also brought the gospel into a pluralistic society where every god was acknowledged, and questioning the beliefs of another was strictly taboo.[9]

This is not to say that rational apologetics are no longer use-

ful—far from it. They still are the best means of convincing many
of the claims of Christ.[10] And as the so-called new atheism makes
its appeal to the masses on the basis of reason, it continues to give
an avenue for a reasoned response.[11] But for most people traditional apologetics become useful at a later point in the process
than they have in the past. Before the faith can be plausibly argued
and the very good reasons to believe be accepted by the hearer, it
must first be embodied over time in real people in a way that is
winsome and convincing.

The term *embodied apologetic* is commonly used among younger
churches, but very little has been said about how we might construct such an apologetic. I will suggest one concrete shape that
such an apologetic might take, and I hope to spur others on to suggest other concrete shapes as well. First though, we need to look
at how people in our culture approach the question of truth.

TRUTH IN A CULTURE OF RADICAL DOUBT

One can certainly make the case that the core issue in our current
cultural shift is epistemology. Questions concerning the nature of
truth and, more typically, of how we discern truth are at the fore-
front of this discussion. Postmoderns are often portrayed as not
believing that truth exists at all, but I find that (at the street level
at least) this is not the case. While belief in truth has not evapo-
rated altogether, we could certainly say that there is a lack of certainty regarding truth claims. In fact, one helpful way to speak of
postmodernity is as a collective loss of confidence in what we are
actually able to know.[12]

Much of this loss of confidence has to do with the means by
which truth is discovered. In the modern era the primary means
of arriving at truth was through reason, logic, presentation of evidence and the scientific method. What has become clearer in the
postmodern shift is that this approach has its limitations. Reason,
it would seem, is not infallible, even when grounded on beliefs we

believe to be basic or foundational. Especially in the case of the younger generations, who have grown up in postmodernity, it is difficult to trust in facts as objective. Life has taught them that what is presented as cold hard fact is often "interpreted fact" that has been shaded to serve someone's agenda. In politics, media, statistics, religion, science and relationships, what has been presented as truth has often been far from true. Even in the sciences, today's incontrovertible fact is on the trash heap tomorrow. The conclusion drawn is that even reason or science are fallible and are subject to both willful and unknowing distortion by those who wield them.[13] What is more, there seem to be realities in our universe that are beyond our ability to explain or describe through the use of these methods. So, while they are not irrational, postmoderns hold to a belief that more than reason alone is needed to arrive at truth.

This skepticism tends to be especially acute in the case of claims that a particular truth, religion or moral teaching is true for everyone, not just for those making the truth claim. Postmoderns are likely to reject the idea that one person's beliefs are equally true for all people, and to pursue alternate means of looking for truth.

For the typical postmodern, personal experience is a key arbiter of truth. Competing truth claims are processed, not as building blocks on a bomb-proof foundation, but on how coherent they are with other beliefs the person holds. Similarly, truth claims are evaluated pragmatically. Something is deemed to be true if it "works" or somehow has beneficial consequences. Factored into both of these approaches are the shared beliefs of that person's immediate community. The community will share experiences and reinforce what is believed to be true.[14]

It is for this reason that traditional apologetics often seem completely lost on postmoderns. Their diminished view of truth makes such apologetics largely irrelevant, and logical arguments may be greeted with a shrug and a "so what."[15] In utilizing an embodied apologetic, we are recognizing the tendency of postmodern people to put more confidence in what they experience, what their immediate community holds as true and what they see "work" than in what merely seems to make sense rationally.

There is a fine balance here that we as believers would be wise to preserve. On the one hand, postmodern thinking makes a valuable contribution when it reminds us that observers are not completely objective; we bring our own biases and distortions to the process of discerning what is true. As believers, we should not need those outside the fold to remind us that sin has distorted our ability to know and to reason, that our use of knowledge is readily bent toward our own self interest, and that what we do know is only partial and incomplete.[16]

Our own Scriptures remind us that every part of us, our reasoning faculties included, has been affected by the Fall (Eph 4:17-18; Rom 8:6-7). God has given us a powerful ability to think, but we must remember that this too has been stained and distorted by sin, and cannot be relied on with ultimate certainty. According to John Calvin (himself a champion of reason), this humility, this yielding of reason to the Holy Spirit and the Scriptures, sets us apart from the world's philosophers. To fully understand the intricacies of our salvation would require us to "transcend the reach of our own intellect."[17] Thus we are called as believers into the ongoing process of renewing our minds and allowing them, along with the rest of our being, to be shaped and transformed by the life of Christ within us (1 Cor 2:16; Rom 12:2; Eph 4:23).

In addition to this tendency to distort, we are limited in what we are able to know. As Paul tells us, life on this side of heaven is much like looking into a poor mirror or through a piece of dark glass (1 Cor 13:12). The very fact that we are finite creatures embodied in flesh and relying on our three-pound brains to figure out the universe should cause us to express truths with great humility.

On the other hand, we must be careful not to overstate the limitations we face in discerning truth. At the end of the day, we must recognize that in Scripture God has given his people the task of knowing him, knowing one another and knowing the world he has placed us in. This task presupposes that God has given us some degree of proficiency in being able to acquire knowledge. We can hold certain things to be true, because, in spite of our limitations "God has given us reason, our five senses, memory, conscience, the heritage of the past, each other's company, and other good gifts" to help us know our world, even if we do so through intellectual models and without perfect objectivity.[18] Indeed, the emerging church will do well to listen to its critics at this point. However truth is understood, arrived at and formulated in a postmodern world, if we are to be biblically faithful followers of Jesus, we must speak of truth with no less confidence than the Scriptures do.

A perspective that recognizes both our ability to know truth and our limitations and biases in doing so might be termed a type of critical realism, chastened rationality or a humble correspondence.[19] According to N. T. Wright, critical realism acknowledges the reality of the thing known (independent of the knower) but also recognizes that the knowledge of this reality is not itself independent of the knower.[20]

Skeptical people, however, need to have those in the church present the gospel in a way that will be heard. We must remember that as missionaries to our culture, we have to approach people where they actually are, not where we wish they were. This points us all the more readily to the need for an apologetic that goes beyond rational arguments and is actively embodied in Christ's people. Philip Kenneson notes, "What our world is waiting for, and what the church seems reluctant to offer, is not more incessant talk about objective truth, but an embodied witness that clearly demonstrates why anyone should care about any of this in the first place."[21]

CONSTRUCTING AN EMBODIED APOLOGETIC

John Stackhouse describes the North American missionary situation well when he says that the biggest problem we face is the "plausibility gap." "Most apologetics throughout Christian history have been directed at the issue of credibility, 'Is it true?' Nowadays, however, we are faced with the prior question, the question of *plausibility*, 'Might it be true? Is Christian argument something I should seriously entertain even for a moment?' "[22] Before our reasons for believing are even considered, we need to address this question of plausibility, and do so in a way that connects our faith to the questions people are asking and the desires they have.

There are three hungers that seem to be particularly close to the surface in our post-Christian society. First, there is a hunger for transcendence. For most, there is some level of awareness that the spiritual world is real, and there is a desire to somehow connect with these transcendent realities. Second, there is a hunger for community. While the hyper-individualism of our culture continues to dominate, it has also awakened a greater awareness of our need to be meaningfully connected to others. Third, there is a hunger for purpose. We live in an affluent time and place in world history, which has helped awaken the reality that we are made for more than simply making and spending money. Among young adults there is a recognition that we are made for a purpose, and we want our lives to count for something.

We in the church should find ourselves challenged by the presence of these hungers, because the gospel addresses all three. Does our worship convey a sense of the transcendent reality of God? Do our congregations manifest love for one another in such a way that we are an appealing community to those outside? Does our teaching convey the significance and purpose that is ours as children of God, called out and sent into the world to fulfill his good purposes?

The embodied apologetic I am fleshing out here corresponds with these hungers, as well as with the ministries of the church. It is an apologetic that is *experiential, communal* and *enacted*. These three facets are interrelated and will have considerable overlap in the church's practice. More will be said about this later, but this kind of apologetic presupposes that evangelism will most often occur as a process, rather than as a one-time event. In Life Covenant Church we are attempting to weave these elements into the way that we structure ourselves, tying the central ministries of the church to these apologetics. We consider our central ministries to be our worship gatherings, expressions of community (such as small groups, mentoring relationships and sharing meals in people's homes), and ministries of compassion. These three ministries are the primary areas we urge our people to participate in, both for their own spiritual formation and as a vehicle for helping their non-Christian friends investigate and participate in the message of Jesus.

Experiential. In a postmodern world where truth is dogged by deep skepticism, experience is often the primary arbiter of truth. What an individual and his or her community experiences is most often what will be considered true. Thus, an embodied apologetic is experiential.

This poses challenges for the church, but I also see tremendous opportunity. The postmodern who desires to encounter that which is real is pursuing a God who will not disappoint. I contend that at its core Christianity is an experiential religion and lends itself very naturally to an experiential apologetic.

In the modern evangelical church, however, experience is suspect—risky at best and deceptive at worst. Granted, experience alone is not a reliable guide, and should not be divorced from either the revelation of Scripture or reason. However, a Christianity that is only cerebral is also misguided. The Christian life is not meant to be an objective pursuit of orthodox doctrine but is embodied in those who follow a Person rather than a dogma. Erwin McManus offers this lament of the church's non-experiential bias:

> Somehow Christianity has become a nonmystical religion. [As currently practiced] it's about a reasonable faith. If we believe the right things, then we are orthodox. Frankly whether we ever actually connect to God or experience His undeniable presence has become incidental, if not irrelevant. We have become believers rather than experiencers.[23]

Moreover, Scripture affirms experience as a form of apologetics. In Scripture our experience of God is an important means by which we can determine whether he is real. The psalmist invites us to "taste and see that the LORD is good" (Ps 34:8). Drawing on the same language, Peter admonishes us to grow up in the Lord, now that we "have tasted that the Lord is good" (1 Pet 2:3). It seems that some part of the process of coming to believe in Christ is experiencing Christ.

Jesus' ministry was characterized by an experiential apologetic. In addition to proclaiming the kingdom of God, Jesus demonstrated its reality through his actions. His healings, exorcisms and miracles are best understood as signs that the kingdom of God was in their midst (Lk 11:20), proving that the message Jesus brought is true. Think of Jesus' early encounter with the fishermen who became his disciples. The miraculous catch of fish that Jesus arranges prompts the astonished Peter to repent and become a follower (Lk 5:9). John writes his Gospel account with an explicit purpose in mind: "that you may believe that Jesus is the Christ, the Son of God, and that by believing you may have life in his name" (Jn 20:31), and he arranges his book around seven "signs" that point to this reality of who Jesus is (Jn 10:38).[24] Jesus expects that his hearers will recognize him as the truth, not just because of his words but because their experience demonstrates his message.

This pattern was continued by Jesus' disciples in the book of Acts. Seldom do you find a proclamation of the gospel without an accompanying experience of the gospel. In nearly every conversion in Acts, the hearers' experience of the gospel is connected with the receipt and progress of the gospel. Acts 14:3 is paradigmatic: "So Paul and Barnabas spent considerable time there, speaking boldly for the Lord, *who confirmed the message of his grace* by enabling them to perform signs and wonders" (emphasis added).[25]

Jesus was explicit in his appeal to experience, and he modeled this approach for his disciples as well. When John the Baptist was gripped by doubt, he sent messengers to ask Jesus if he truly was the Messiah. Jesus responded by appealing to the actions that John and others had experienced: "Go back and report to John what you have seen and heard" (Lk 7:22). When two potential followers inquired where Jesus was staying (an idiom reflecting the desire to explore becoming his disciples), Jesus responded with an invitation to experience: "Come . . . and you will see" (Jn 1:39).[26] Having been invited by Jesus to see who he is, Andrew invited his brother Peter to investigate Jesus in the same way (Jn 1:41). The proof that Jesus offered was an experience of himself.

In the same way, Philip took Jesus' own words as he invited Nathanael to "come and see" whether Jesus was indeed the Messiah (Jn 1:46). Nathanael was not disappointed; Jesus responded to his inquiry by letting him experience a minor demonstration of his power, with the promise of greater and more convincing proofs to follow. "You will see," said Jesus, " 'heaven open and the angels of God ascending and descending on' the Son of Man." These potential disciples would not know the truth about Jesus until they actually experienced him. At this point in the text (Jn 1:51), the verb shifts from singular to plural, indicating that not only Nathanael but the other disciples, and implicitly, John's readers, would experience things that would point them to the reality of Jesus.[27]

How can we as a church offer an experiential apologetic to those investigating the faith? While all three of the ministry structures mentioned earlier have an element of experience, one that particularly lends itself to an experiential apologetic is the worship gathering.

Worship evangelism is a particularly important means of proclaiming the gospel to postmodern people. Genuine experiences of worship (as seen in song, prayer, God's Word taught and proclaimed, art, personal storytelling, participation in the Lord's Supper, baptism, etc.), in addition to their importance for the spiritual formation of believers, are a powerful apologetic for Christ. My own experience mirrors that of so many I have known who have encountered the undeniable reality of God's power and beauty embodied in his people as they engaged in worship.

In worship, the truth of the gospel is proclaimed and acted out. For those who are skeptical of truth claims, witnessing God meeting his people in a sincere, passionate experience of worship often proves more powerful than a host of logical evidences for the reality of the faith.[28] The worship in many young churches is well-suited to have this kind of apologetic side effect, because these churches typically react strongly against entertainment worship, long for a genuine experience of God's presence and focus on the transcendent otherness of God.

Communal. In addition to being experienced, an embodied apologetic will be communal. That is, the message of Christ will be more readily accepted when it is embodied not just in an individual but in a community of Christians who are committed to being shaped into the image of Christ, loving one another and serving their world. This is especially true as we are able to move beyond merely showing Christian community to others and actually allowing our non-Christian friends to participate in this community. Relating his observation of how postmoderns normally come to faith, Doug Pagitt says, "In many ways, becoming Christian is much like learning our native language; we pick it up when we are immersed in it."[29]

In a postmodern world where experience is often the primary gauge for measuring truth, the experience of an individual's community confirms what a person believes to be true. When an experience is shared by others, it moves from being "my story" to "our story" and becomes more plausible. In addition to this, postmodern people have a deeply felt need for community. The hyper-individualism and family fragmentation of late modernity have left the postmodern generations with a great hunger to be connected meaningfully to others. This affords great opportunity to the church that wants to minister to these generations, particularly as the church works to live out a caring, authentic sense of community. The church itself becomes a powerful apologetic as it strives to be what it is supposed to be.

In the New Testament this communal aspect of witness is quite evident. Jesus tells his followers that the world will know they are his disciples by the way they love one another (Jn 13:35). In saying this, Jesus is inviting the unbelieving world to use the quality of our love as a basis to decide on the reality of the gospel. Similarly, Jesus states that our connectedness to him and to one another (Jn 17:21, 23) is proof to the world that Jesus was sent into the world by the Father, and that the Father loves us the way he loves the Son. In being united with God and one another, the church serves as the world's first taste of what life in God's kingdom will be like.

The early church testifies to the reality of Jesus' words. In Acts 2:42-47 and 4:32-37, we see how the community served as witness to the realities it proclaimed to the people. In the second century, Tertullian quoted pagan people coming to faith who commented not on the rational arguments the church offered but instead said, "See how they love one another!"[30] The message of Christ is most compelling when coming from believers whose lives reflect the reality of the message and from churches who reflect the reality of Christ. "The church's mission is to *show the world what it looks like when a community of people live under the reign of God.*"[31]

A similar emphasis is seen in the Old Testament book of Ezekiel. "The nations will know that I am the LORD, declares the Sovereign LORD, when I am proved holy through you before their eyes" (Ezek 36:23). God has declared that he will prove he is holy and that the unconvinced will know he is God, not through his actions alone but through the actions of his people.[32]

In addition to the church's actions serving as an apologetic, the early church made appeals for their claims to truth in a communal fashion. The early church presented its collective witness of the risen Christ as evidence of the reality of the faith. The nature of New Testament witness is that a community, not just one or two individuals, bore witness to the reality that Jesus was alive. John, Peter and Paul appeal to this community of witnesses ("We have seen" in 1 Jn 1:1-3; 1 Cor 15:5-8; 2 Pet 1:16-19; cf. Lk 1:1-4; "we" in Jn 21:24). For most relativists, a rational argument might be dismissed, but a person's story is generally held in high regard. As believers, we bring a story of encountering the living God. Even more important, we are a part of a community that brings its stories as well.

What will it look like in the local church to present the world with a communal apologetic? How do we help people experience the love of Christ, and not just experience the church as strangers in a crowd or as spectators at an event? The structures in the church that seem best suited to this are the smaller expressions of community that foster connectedness. At Life these take shape in small groups (which meet for prayer, Bible study, service and to give inquirers a safe place to investigate), "front porch events" (which foster social connectedness at a very nonthreatening level) and sharing meals in people's homes.

In a communal apologetic, evangelism has less to do with inviting people to events and more with inviting them into our lives. This means churched people will be encouraged to greater involvement outside the church, cultivating friendships that serve as bridges to allow others to investigate the faith community. As they are immersed in the community of believers, those investigating are given a venue to see, hear and feel the reality of the faith as it is lived out.

In addition, relying on the church to embody the message means that we will take seriously the task of helping our people grow in their faith. We will become an authentic community, effective as an apologetic, only as God transforms us into the image of Christ. For this reason intentional spiritual formation will figure prominently in our strategy for evangelism as well as discipleship. As Dallas Willard says:

> The way to get as many people into heaven as you can is to get heaven into as many people as you can—that is, to follow the path of genuine spiritual transformation or full-throttle discipleship to Jesus Christ. When we are counting up results we also need to keep in mind the multitudes of people (surrounded by churches) who will not be in heaven because they have never, to their knowledge, seen the reality of Christ in a living human being.[33]

In pursuing this approach, we will construct an apologetic that is communal.

Enacted. An embodied apologetic is experienced, takes place in the context of community, and is enacted by those in the community. Too often, Christianity is seen by those on the outside (and often those on the inside as well) as concerned only with believing the right things, attending church and avoiding certain behaviors. What a contrast this is to the kingdom announcement of Jesus! The church serves as a sign, instrument and first taste of God's kingdom.[34] When the church lives as it is called to live, the world receives a powerful apologetic: a glimpse of what it looks like when God reigns in the world.

In the Sermon on the Mount, Jesus told his followers that they are the salt of the earth and the light of the world (Mt 5:13-14). In a sense, Jesus is calling believers to serve as an enacted apologetic. "Let your light shine before others, that they may see your good deeds and glorify your Father in heaven" (Mt 5:16). Doing good in the name of Jesus will serve to convince the world of the praise-worthy nature of the Christian God.

This ethos carried over into the early church. In Acts the church's apologetic was enacted in the distribution of food to needy widows. This ministry existed alongside prayer and the ministry of God's Word, and the result was an increase in the number of disciples, with a large number of Jewish priests among those who chose to follow Jesus (Acts 6:1-7; cf. Gal 2:10).

Similarly, Peter points to the conduct of the church as an apologetic to an unbelieving world. Peter reminds his hearers that they are a chosen people, deeply loved and called by God to declare his greatness. They are the people of God, recipients of his mercy and, by extension, conduits of his mercy. Peter urges them to remember that they are citizens of another world, and, as such, to have no business pursuing sinful desires (1 Pet 2:9-11). Finally, Peter exhorts them, "Be careful how you live among your unbelieving neighbors. Even if they accuse you of doing wrong, they will see your honorable behavior, and *they will believe and give honor to God* when he judges the world" (1 Pet 2:12 NLT, emphasis added). The good deeds of the church, lived out in the world's presence, will demonstrate the reality of the message we proclaim.

In a second century letter to Caesar Hadrian, the Christian

apologist Aristides cites as evidence for the faith the way the Christians love their enemies, live with honesty, care for the needs of strangers and even fast so they will have enough money to feed the poor. He concludes his letter with this marvelous statement: "Such, O King . . . is their manner of life . . . and verily this is a new people, and there is something divine in the midst of them."[35]

When our apologetic is enacted, it answers the postmodernist's question, Does it work? As the world around us looks at the end results of a belief to see whether it is true, the church that enacts its apologetic will pass the pragmatic test of truth.

While our faith is certainly enacted in our worship gatherings and expressions of community, our primary vehicle for an enacted apologetic are our ministries of compassion and justice. When we provide medicine and education for those with HIV/AIDS, when we build housing for the poor with organizations like Habitat for Humanity, when we offer food and clean clothes to the homeless, when we serve our city's schools through improvement projects— we are demonstrating that our faith works. And postmoderns are hungry to make a difference in their world and are open to participating in these kinds of events alongside Christians. Engaging seekers in Christian action creates opportunity for dialogue about the faith and is persuasive in our case for the reality of the faith.

In addition to changing perceptions of the Christian faith in general, ministries of compassion change people's perceptions of the particular person bringing the message as well. It is important to recognize that to our spiritual friends with whom we share Christ, we are not (at first) who we are, but who they think we are.[36] Until we have shaken loose whatever stereotypes they have attached to Christians, our message will not be heard in context. Engaging in ministries of compassion sets the words of Jesus in a context that mirrors the heart of Jesus and allows the hearer to see the reality of the message as it is acted out. Brian McLaren sums this up well:

I firmly believe that the top question of the new century and new millennium is not just whether Christianity is rational, credible, and essentially true (all of which I believe it is), but whether it can be powerful, redemptive, authentic, and good, whether it can change lives, demonstrate reconciliation and community, serve as a catalyst for the kingdom, and lead to a desirable future. The drama must be played out on the local level, in communities of people who live by the gospel.[37]

CONCLUSION

The mission field in which we find ourselves is marked by deep skepticism over truth and a strong adherence to religious pluralism. This requires that our apologetic be embodied and not merely rational. In practice, I envision an embodied apologetic as being experiential, communal and enacted. These dimensions are related to three God-given hungers that are particularly close to the surface for postmoderns.

Apologetic	Experiential	Communal	Enacted
Need	Transcendence	Community	Purpose

Figure 1.1. Elements of an embodied apologetic

As those who would seek to engage a postmodern world with the gospel, our intention is to weave such an apologetic into the fabric of church life by tying it to the way we structure ourselves for ministry. Before we look at the church structures though, we will take a biblical and theological look at the nature of the church's missionary task and the ministry of disciplemaking.

2

Same Wine, Different Skin

I have become all things to all people
so that by all possible means I might save some.

1 CORINTHIANS 9:22

Mission is not primarily an activity of the church,
but an attribute of God. God is a missionary God.

DAVID J. BOSCH, *TRANSFORMING MISSION*

A few years ago I was invited to speak at a missions conference sponsored by a network of churches with large global missions programs. A friend was speaking on the global aspect of missions, and my job was to address the church's local mission.

They started out as a wonderfully receptive audience, as missions groups so often are. In the session on global missions, people smiled, nodded their approval and were visibly enthusiastic. But when I began talking about integrating some of those same methods at home, the energy seemed to drain out of the room (first thought: *Wow. Am I just lame compared to the last speaker?*). Many of the smiles disappeared, eyebrows were raised, and I even saw a few people cross their arms, lock eyes with me and shake their heads. During the question-and-answer session, objections popped up one after the next. "We can't do those things here. Do you know what that would mean for our children's programs? We wouldn't want to approach worship that way. It's okay for us to disciple that way overseas, but not here." When I gently pointed out that I hadn't suggested anything different than what we had all been celebrating in our global efforts, an uncomfortable silence settled over the room.

I was shocked by their reaction. If there was any group that I thought would be eager to apply mission methods at home, this would be it. There were some, of course, who were enthusiastic about it, but the general attitude of the group was somewhere between resistant and hostile. But it's not just them, of course—I am part of the problem too. If we were being entirely honest, we would all admit to experiencing this discomfort. We understand that the church is meant to carry out the mission of God, and may even be quite passionate about it. But our enthusiasm is often tempered when the mission comes too close to threatening an aspect of church life that we hold dear.

On the mission field we take for granted that we must shift our methods to bring people the gospel in ways they will understand. In fact, most churches would be unwilling to support missionaries who were not interested in learning the language and customs of those they want to reach, and we look in shocked amazement at the compounds and colonies that missionaries in previous centuries employed in their work. But to think in these terms as we look at our own culture can feel quite threatening. As seasoned missiologist and professor Eddie Gibbs wryly observes, "The reality is that the mission compound, which we have abandoned as a viable method in global missions, now exists in the U.S. in the form of the local church."[1]

THE CHURCH AS GOD'S MISSIONARY PEOPLE

Somewhere along the line there was a split between our theology of church and our theology of mission. "Church" became the building on the corner where we worship on Sundays and hold an occasional potluck. "Mission" became an activity that happens somewhere else, usually by someone else. Rather than seeing the church as missional in nature and existing for the good of the world, we came to see the church as existing for our benefit and missions for the benefit of others. The church was a place that, in the words of renowned missiologist Lesslie Newbigin, "approved of 'missions' but was not itself the mission."[2]

This split in our understanding of church and mission has influenced how the church perceives its identity and purpose. In its healthier expression the church exists so that God's people might glorify him.[3] In its less healthy (and arguably more common) expression, the church exists to serve me, the churchgoer. The primary concern becomes whether or not my needs (as I perceive them) are being met. If I come to the conclusion that a given congregation is not meeting my needs (an inevitable conclusion, by the way, if this is my mindset), then I find a new congregation in which to repeat the cycle. As Christians, we are reduced to consumers, and the church is reduced to "a vendor of religious services and goods."[4] Erwin McManus sums up this shift: "Our motto degenerated from 'We are the church, here to serve a lost and dying world' to 'What does the church have to offer me?' "[5]

In the New Testament we find no such split between church and mission. The church exists as the beloved people of God, called out of the world as his children and sent back into it as his authorized ambassadors. The church is the worshiping community of God's missionary people.

If we take seriously the decline of the church in America and our vocation as God's missionary people, then we must begin to approach our own culture less like Sunday churchgoers and more like missionaries in a post-Christian world. I will focus on two aspects of this: first on contextualization, and then in the following two chapters, on what it means to make disciples.

CONTEXTUALIZATION: CULTURAL RELEVANCE IS NOT OPTIONAL

Missionaries speak of bringing the gospel in the "heart language" of a given culture. It is not enough to simply proclaim the gospel like one would at home and then walk away, hoping that they get it. The task of every missionary is to understand the culture to be reached and to bring the undiluted gospel to that culture in a form that will be understandable to the hearers. This process is known as contextualization.

Michael Frost and Alan Hirsch define contextualization as "the dynamic process whereby the constant message of the gospel interacts with specific, relative human situations."[6] Sri Lankan pastor-theologian Ajith Fernando says contextualization has occurred "when the presentation and outworking of the gospel is done in a manner appropriate to the context in which it is found."[7] As a working definition, missionaries contend that contextualization has been carried out effectively when the gospel "offends for the right reasons and not for the wrong ones."[8]

It is important for us to recognize that the gospel is always presented in a particular packaging. When we proclaim the good news of Jesus, we do not do so in a form that is culturally neutral. Lesslie Newbigin says, "We must start with the basic fact that there is no such thing as a pure gospel if by that is meant something which is not embodied in a culture. . . . Every interpretation of the gospel is embodied in some cultural form."[9] It is important that we make this distinction between content and container. To change the way the gospel is presented does not mean we are changing the gospel itself. When we fail to recognize this, we end up making monuments out of our methods (for the sake of preserving the gospel), while, ironically, the gospel we treasure becomes less clear to those with whom we would share it.

CONTEXTUALIZATION IN THE NEW TESTAMENT

Contextualization follows the pattern of the incarnation and the model set by the New Testament church. In Christ, God performs an unrepeatable feat of contextualization in taking on human form. For Jesus, becoming human also meant taking on the particular cultural garb of his environment. He came not as a generic human being but as a Jewish male, wearing Jewish clothes, speaking Aramaic and living by the cultural values of first-century Israel. As Ron Martoia quips, it would have done Jesus little good to come speaking French.[10]

Reflecting on the incarnation, Paul highlights Christ's humility, servanthood and unwavering obedience to the Father as a model for Christ's followers (Phil 2:1-11). Following Jesus into new environs today requires us to imitate his humility, to be willing to surrender our preferences for the joy of the mission and to adapt ourselves to those we wish to reach.

In the book of Acts we see both the struggles and joys that the earliest churches experienced as the gospel spread. Jesus called them to carry the message to Jerusalem and Judea (their same culture), Samaria (a similar culture), and to the ends of the earth (very different cultures). The New Testament records the growing pains the church experienced as it faithfully brought the gospel to these differing settings. Paul summarizes his missionary philosophy in 1 Corinthians:

> Though I am free and belong to no one, I have made myself a slave to everyone, to win as many as possible. To the Jews I became like a Jew, to win the Jews. To those under the law I became like one under the law (though I myself am not under the law), so as to win those under the law. To those not having the law I became like one not having the law (though I am not free from God's law but am under Christ's law), so as to win those not having the law. To the weak I became weak, to win the weak. *I have become all things to all people so that by all possible means I might save some.* I do all

this for the sake of the gospel, that I may share in its blessings. (1 Cor 9:19-23, emphasis added)

In Acts 17:16-34 we have the New Testament's most detailed
example of what Paul's philosophy looks like in practice. Prior to
Acts 17 the bulk of Paul's ministry takes place in the local synagogue or with some other gathering of Jews and God-fearing
Greeks. In Acts 14:1 Paul and Barnabas go "as usual" to the local
synagogue at Iconium, and in Thessalonica they begin to proclaim
Jesus in the synagogue, which Luke describes as Paul's "custom"
(Acts 17:2). Paul would engage his hearers with Old Testament
teachings about the Messiah, then share Jesus of Nazareth as the
fulfillment of those Scriptures.

In Athens, Paul finds his primary ministry taking place in the
Greek marketplace. Paul's message is met with a surprising reaction: "What is this babbler trying to say?" (Act 17:18). I'm always
amazed by this—they call Paul, the ultralogical author of Romans,
a "babbler"! "He seems to be advocating foreign gods," they go on to
say. "You are bringing some strange ideas to our ears" (vv. 18, 20).

In other words, it is not just that the Athenians disagree with
Paul. They don't understand him well enough to either accept or
reject what he is saying! Paul's presentation of the gospel is essentially a Jewish one, and it is lost on his Greek hearers.[11]

Paul is given another chance to share the message, this time in
front of the Areopagus, and his approach is considerably different.
His response to this situation is a great model of contextualization.

Finding common ground. First, Paul begins by identifying with
a touch point in the Athenian's culture. As a faithful Jew, Paul is
appalled at the idol worship he sees in the city (Acts 17:16). Yet, in
spite of his intense feelings, he sees in this the reality of the Athenians' religious fervor, as well as an opportunity to connect the
gospel to their preexisting beliefs. Paul draws attention to the al-

tar they have devoted to an unknown god, and announces that the god they have worshiped anonymously has an identity which Paul will reveal to them (v. 23). In doing so, Paul calls attention to a need the Athenians have already acknowledged, then proposes a remedy.

Paul is unafraid to find areas of agreement between his faith in Jesus and the religious beliefs of those he seeks to evangelize. Augustine is credited with the oft-repeated phrase, "All truth is God's truth," and I think Paul would agree with this statement as well. We must remember that as we engage our unbelieving friends in dialogue, elements of their belief systems and worldviews will be true. Rather than dismissing their thinking as wholly incorrect, we would do well to follow Paul's example and build on those areas where our beliefs coincide. Without touch points it will be difficult for those hearing this new message to truly grasp it. "None of us can begin to understand anything except by relating it to what we already know, and therefore to the models which have hitherto organized our experience."[12] As missionaries, we need to seriously examine our host culture to find the touch points which will make the gospel understandable.

Our post-Christian world, like Athens, is very religious. The religious landscape is covered with an array of beliefs, syncretized and sanitized to fit popular tastes. This religious diversity will create increased opportunities for us to point out areas of agreement between their faith and ours. Tim Downs notes that Paul could just as easily have highlighted the enormous areas of disagreement between himself and the Athenians (as the church in America is prone to do), but he chose to build on their agreements rather than their arguments.[13] In a postmodern world, there is no shortage of common ground.

In my own ministry I have found the spiritual disciplines to be one such area of common ground. Postmoderns are hungry for experiential forms of spirituality and often have a great interest in spiritual practices. One young lady I met described herself as deeply spiritual and subscribed to a modified Buddhist pantheism. The touch point that opened up our dialogue was her experimentation with Eastern meditation. When I told her that I regularly practiced meditation (in its Christian forms) she was shocked, as her impression of Christianity was that it was only about holding certain beliefs and not about the actual practice of spirituality. This became the basis for our further discussions about Christ. In the course of our relationship, she tried Ignatian meditation on gospel passages and read Brother Lawrence.

When my wife and I were going through Lamaze classes, one of our classmates was trying to become a seminar teacher on New Age spirituality. "Really!" I said. "I've done a lot of teaching on spiritual practices too." He was intrigued, and our mutual interest in spirituality led to a relationship and a level of comfort for him to open up about why he had abandoned Christianity, and to ask whether Jesus would still accept him on the path he had now taken.

The world is hungry for God, and clues to this hunger will appear in culture. Finding areas of common ground will enable missionaries to speak to that hunger.

Looking for God at work. Second, Paul recognizes God's fingerprints in Athenian culture. "I see that in every way you are very religious," Paul begins (Acts 17:22). Not only does Paul see touch points between their religion and Christianity, but he recognizes that God is already working in their culture to draw these people toward himself (see Jn 6:44). Knowing this, Paul is observant ("As I walked around and *looked carefully* at your objects of worship . . ." [v. 23]), looking for opportunities to share the gospel in ways his hearers will understand.

Paul understands that God arrived in Athens before Paul did. In a remarkable statement of the extent of God's pursuit of his people, Paul declares, "God did this [determined the exact times and places where everyone would live] so that they would seek him and perhaps reach out for him and find him, though he is not far from any one of us" (v. 27). Here is one of the most marvelous statements in Scripture about God being a missionary. Not only does God pursue us, he has prearranged our circumstances in such a way that each of us would be most inclined to seek and perhaps find him. Though our hearts' propensity is to turn away from our Creator, God has stacked the deck in our favor. Long before a gospel witness ever arrives, God is at work in the lives of those who will come to faith, to the point of placing people in the time and place in history that will best encourage their seeking him.

A similar point is made during Paul and Barnabas's ministry in Lystra. "He has not left himself without testimony: He has shown kindness by giving you rain from heaven and crops in their seasons; he provides you with plenty of food and fills your hearts with joy" (Acts 14:17). Paul recognizes that long before he arrived, God was at work among these people, revealing himself, leading them to repentance with his kindness (Rom 2:4) and preparing them to one day receive the gospel. We are reminded also of the words of assurance Jesus spoke to Paul in Corinth: "Do not be afraid; keep on speaking, do not be silent. For I am with you, and no one is going to attack and harm you, because I have many people in this city" (Acts 18:9-10). This city was receiving its first gospel witness, yet Jesus assures Paul that he has gone before him, preparing people's hearts to receive the good news.

One of the most fascinating studies in missions is the occurrence of redemptive analogies. There are abundant stories in the history of missions of encountering unreached people groups whose preparation to receive the gospel can only be described as supernatural. In local customs and traditions, folk stories and legends, linguistic elements, and even in the prophecies of local shamans, foreshadowings of the gospel spring to life when it is presented. Seeing these parallels, early Christians often regarded pagan religions as *preparatio evangelica*, a preparation for the gospel God had embedded in the culture.[14]

The missionary lives in tension here, as Scripture primarily portrays pagan religions as idolatrous and demonic (1 Cor 10:18-21; Rev 9:20), while in a few instances the religions (or at least aspects of a religion) are presented as an honest yet incomplete expression of a peoples' search for God (Gen 14:18; Acts 14:17; 17; Rom 1:20-23; 2:14-15). We must hold these two aspects in tension, remembering on the one hand that a given religion may contain truths that point people toward God, and on the other hand that the "world of the religions is the world of the demonic."[15] This should not be seen as a capitulation to pluralism, but as a reminder that truth is truth, regardless of its origin.

I find it helpful when I'm talking with friends who are far from God to ask about times when they think they have experienced God as real or have sensed that God is somehow reaching out to them. I have yet to encounter a person who does not have some story to relate (including some who moments before assured me they were hardened atheists). From surviving accidents that should have been fatal to having dreams where Jesus spoke to them, many carry memories of times when they believe they have experienced God. Much of our task as evangelists is to help our unbelieving friends identify the work that God is already doing in their lives.

Arguing to the Scriptures. Third, Paul relates the truths of the gospel to sources the Athenians are already familiar with. " 'For in him we live and move and have our being.' As some of your own poets have said, 'We are his offspring'" (Acts 17:28). Here Paul quotes the Athenians' own Epicurean and Stoic poets and philosophers to bolster his case.[16]

Knowing that his audience respects these thinkers, Paul enlists them in order to call the Athenian views into question and make his own message more plausible. The first quotation (understood in a pantheistic sense by the Athenians) is used by Paul to affirm that God is separate from, yet near, his creation (v. 27). The second quotation highlights that since God is humanity's Creator, it would be foolish for the Athenians to think of themselves as creating him with gold or silver or stone (v. 29). It likely also serves the purpose of reinforcing that all people come from "one nation of men," contrary to the Athenian boast that they sprung up from the soil of their homeland and were therefore unique.[17]

We see here glimpses of a strategy Curtis Chang elaborates on in his study of contextualization. He sees in the New Testament, as well as in Augustine and Aquinas, a pattern that is very instructive (a process he refers to as "taking every thought captive"). The first step in this process is to enter the challenger's story. Here we meet the rival story on its own terms, choosing to operate within the challenger's worldview. The second step is retelling the story. The rival story is modified and reinterpreted, using the story's own language, to highlight and magnify those aspects that dovetail with the gospel. Third, the retold story is "captured" within the gospel narrative. In other words, the gospel story becomes the larger story as it subsumes and explains the rival story. The rival worldview ends up being explained within the biblical worldview.[18]

Paul's familiarity with the beliefs of his Epicurean and Stoic listeners allows him to effectively enter their story and address their idolatry from within. By telling the gospel story in the manner he does and by utilizing their own poets and philosophers in doing so, he modifies and retells the Athenian story from a Christian perspective. This retelling of their story in light of the gospel story addresses and confronts the Athenian beliefs about creation, idols, God's relation to his creatures, the Epicurean contention that God is uninvolved in human affairs, and their lack of belief in a resurrection. The gospel becomes the "bigger" story, and their story is captured within a biblical worldview.

Note that Paul does not quote from the Old Testament as he would have in a Jewish setting. He wisely recognizes that his hearers do not recognize the Jewish Scriptures as authoritative and consequently does not utilize them as such. At the same time, his message is thoroughly biblical. His lack of biblical quotations should not be taken as any doubt on Paul's part as to the power of the Scriptures, but rather as an attempt to introduce the truth of Scripture to his hearers in a way that they will accept. Rather than arguing *from* the Scriptures (as he does with the Jews), he takes a roundabout journey through Greek philosophy and argues *to* the Scriptures.

This is critical to the way we approach missions in our cultural setting as well. We must recognize that in bringing the gospel to a postmodern world, we are encountering people who are increasingly unfamiliar with the biblical story, and who do not recognize the Bible as an authoritative source. At times we may find it helpful, as Paul did, to appeal to the culture's own poets and philosophers, and to argue to the Scriptures rather than from them.

Who are the poets and philosophers that our culture looks to? Ravi Zacharias makes the case that they are our artists and songwriters; I would add makers of television and film. We need to learn to make an ally of pop culture. The postmodern generations are extremely well-versed in and deeply affected by popular culture. Where earlier generations may have read or sought out leading authorities to make sense of their world, the emerging generations are far more likely to look to film, music and television, not just for entertainment but as "meaning-making systems."[19] These forms figure prominently in postmoderns' attempts to form a worldview. Rather than look at these media as an adversary or attempt to create Christian imitations to compete against them, we are wise to become conversant in the stories being told and the views being expressed in popular culture. As Chuck Smith Jr. puts it, "We do not have to take God into popular culture since He is already there, giving people impressions, revealing shades of His truth, and leaving His fingerprints."[20] Chang comments, "Movies convey the stories of postmoderns in a way no other medium does. . . . Entering our challenger's stories will mean entering the movie theater with them."[21]

As we do this, the church will accomplish two things. First, we will gain a greater understanding of our mission field. By familiarizing ourselves with popular culture we will learn to communicate in the language of the culture, enter into the questions the culture is asking, and be able to enter the dialogue in ways that are understandable. Second, we will be able to look for and work with the ways God is already showing up in popular culture. When we read Peter's admonition for us to "always be prepared to give an answer to everyone who asks you to give the reason for the hope that you have" (1 Pet 3:15), it is important that we recognize, as Paul did, that this includes familiarity with the worldview of our hearers.

In engaging the culture in this way, there are two extremes for us to avoid. The first is to think that exposing ourselves to pop culture does not affect us. Even as we engage the culture, we must use discernment, prayerfully forge convictions about what is and is not appropriate, and keep from sin. The other extreme is to think that any engagement with culture will contaminate us, and avoid it altogether. Again, Chuck Smith Jr. sums it up brilliantly: "The truth is that there is no place in popular culture a Christian cannot enter provided we know who we are, we do not forget our mission, and we refuse to indulge in anything prohibited by Scripture."[22]

Starting the story further back. Fourth, it is important to note that Paul's message starts "further back" with the Greeks than it does with the Jews. When sharing Jesus with an audience of Jews or God-fearers, Paul was able to appeal to their shared history and Scriptures to persuade them that Jesus was the promised Messiah

(Acts 13:15-41; 17:2-3, 10-11). He and his hearers shared a common worldview, an assumed monotheism, faith in the God of Israel, an understanding of his covenants and the expectation of a coming kingdom and Messiah.[23]

In Athens (as in Iconium), no such common ground exists. Paul's hearers subscribe to a different view of the universe and worship different gods. Consequently, Paul cannot meaningfully proclaim that the Messiah has come without first introducing the Athenians to the God of Israel. He does this by proclaiming to them God as Creator of the world and all that is in it, and as the one who rules as Lord over heaven and earth (Acts 17:24; compare Acts 14:15). He describes God as the sustainer of life, who does not need to have food brought to him or to be housed in a temple like an idol, because "he himself gives everyone life and breath and everything else" (Acts 17:25). Paul describes God as the great pursuer of humanity as well. He has laid out the life circumstances of each person such that they might seek and reach out to him (Acts 17:26-28). Finally, Paul describes God as the great judge who requires humans to repent from their idolatry and who will bring justice to the world (Acts 17:29-31). It is only at this last point, when a basic understanding of who God is has been established, that Jesus is introduced, not with the term *Messiah* (which is so meaningful to the Jews), but as "the man he has appointed," the one whom God raised from the dead (Acts 17:31).

For most of our country's history, a basic understanding of the Christian God could be assumed. When we spoke of God, we could safely assume the hearer would picture a sort of personal, monotheistic Creator. A majority of Americans had some church background, had gone to Sunday school as children and operated out of a marginally biblical worldview. Bible stories and scriptural references were common enough in cultural discourse that biblical allusions would be recognized in the public square. Most people also had some basic understanding of who Jesus is, and consequently he needed only minimal introduction.

This is illustrated well by the widely used "Four Spiritual Laws" tract. The booklet opens by stating that "God loves you and has a wonderful plan for your life." No explanation is given for what type of being this God is, whether or not there is only one God, if God is a force or a person, and so forth. The evangelist is free to launch immediately into a discussion of God's love and our broken relationship with him. Similarly, Jesus is presented with little identification, and the booklet moves directly into Christ's work on our behalf and the importance of receiving him as Savior.

In many ways this kind of evangelism is a carryover of revival evangelism in the eighteenth and nineteenth centuries. Virtually everyone was culturally Christian, and nominalism was the real issue evangelism addressed.[24] A biblical worldview and an understanding of Christ was the norm, and evangelism consisted of calling people to commit to something they most likely already believed in on some level. People were essentially acting on what they already knew, as opposed to encountering information that they did not previously have. In this milieu, evangelistic tools like the altar call were developed, and seeds were planted for the mass evangelistic rallies and tract evangelism of the twentieth century.[25]

In a heavily Christianized culture this kind of evangelism made sense, and the evangelistic tools which rose to prominence in that time were well-suited for their context. Evangelism became event oriented (in both its mass and personal forms), and the revival model lent itself to a sort of sales approach, complete with an emphasis on "closing the deal." Immediate decisions were called for and, as most were making a decision based on a lifetime of exposure to Christianity, immediate decisions became the norm. However, as the culture began to shift in the later twentieth century, these methods made less sense and were less effective, particularly among those who were not already nominally Christian.[26]

In our shifting cultural context, we can no longer assume that our hearers will have a biblical worldview, believe in a monotheistic Creator God or have any knowledge of Jesus. As Paul did with the Athenians, we need to begin the story further back, describing the Creator before we speak about Christ. Eddie Gibbs suggests that in a post-Christian context, we should "assume people know nothing about the Bible and the Good News until [we] have evidence to the contrary."[27] My colleague Scott Buetzow has noted that most presentations of the gospel start with the Fall and end with redemption. He suggests bookending these points with creation and restoration, which both starts the story further back and pushes it forward into a fuller conclusion.

In addition, evangelism as a decision-oriented event becomes far less effective in the absence of a Christian worldview. Whether in evangelistic crusades, rallies or the sharing of a tract with a stranger, the "close-the-deal" approach has born far less fruit with postmodern people.[28] We must face the fact that evangelism in the United States is increasingly a crosscultural engagement, and we need to treat it as such.

It may be noteworthy that Luke reports a less than overwhelming response that day (Acts 17:34). Those who were willing to respond immediately to the message (to the "event" of Paul's preaching that day) were less than Paul normally experienced in more Jewish contexts. However, there were those who wanted to hear more and who chose to continue to be exposed to Paul's teaching (Acts 17:32).

Preaching without compromise. Finally, it is very important for us to recognize that Paul does not water down the message of Christ. "This is the classic task of the cross-cultural missionary," write Frost and Hirsch, "to engage culture without compromising the gospel."[29] The temptation to soften the harder edges of the gospel is always present, and critics of the emerging church do us a great service in offering cautions in this regard.

We see here that Paul is very forthright in confronting idolatry and stating unapologetically that God "commands all people everywhere to repent" (Acts 17:30; see also Acts 14:15). He does not hesitate to offer the resurrection of Jesus as evidence for his message, even though this is a laughable concept in the minds of his hearers (Acts 17:31-32).

We misunderstand contextualization if we see it as an attempt to make the gospel more palatable. It would be hard to imagine anyone accusing Paul of somehow sanitizing or sugarcoating the message. The gospel is offensive, and the point of contextualization is not to change that. Rather, the idea is to speak the gospel in the heart language of the hearer. (With tongue firmly in cheek Michael Slaughter says, "The gospel is offensive, but we need to put it in a language so that people will recognize they've been offended!")[30]

Nor should people misunderstand contextualization as a way of better marketing the church. Eddie Gibbs distinguishes between marketing the church and contextualizing the church. The contextualized church "represents a serious attempt to engage with the cultural setting in which the local church is endeavoring to bear witness," whereas the market-driven church "signifies a church that tailors its message and employs any gimmick in order to attract a crowd."[31] Os Guinness cautions, "Joining people where they are at is only the first step in the process, not the last," and "when the audience and not the message is sovereign, the good news of Jesus Christ is no longer the end, but just the means."[32] The danger of accommodation is a real one, and we must be careful that the message we are delivering is that of the Bible and not a dressed-up version of what our culture would like to hear.

Jesus is difficult. He demands our complete allegiance and warns those who would follow him to count the cost before doing so (Lk 14:28-31). The role of the missionary is not to water down or sanitize the message, but to bring it in all its starkness in the best way possible. If we compromise the message, we must conclude that our attempts at contextualization have failed. Yet at the same time we cannot be content to present the gospel without any thought of context and simply say, "I did my part—I gave them the Word," if in fact we have not made real efforts to bring that Word to people in ways that are understandable and winsome, "full of grace, seasoned with salt" (Col 4:6).

POST-NEW TESTAMENT CONTEXTUALIZATION

Contextualization did not end with the New Testament church. While its practice has ebbed and flowed in the church's history, contextualization can be seen as the church surged into new areas and experienced significant awakenings and turning points.

In the second-century *Epistle to Diognetus* the writer notes that "Christians are not distinguished from the rest of humanity by country, language, or custom." Indeed, whether they live in a Greek or barbarian city, they "follow the local customs in dress and food and other aspects of life," while living a lifestyle that distinguishes them morally as people whose true citizenship is in heaven.[33] In the fourth and fifth centuries, contextualization was a hallmark of St. Patrick and successive missions to Ireland.[34] In the sixth century, Pope Gregory the Great gave a directive that missions should be carried on with contextualization in mind.[35] This principle was notably picked up by the Jesuits in the seventeenth century, who were urged to exercise caution in importing their own customs into the churches they established. A key document asks, "What could be more absurd than to transport France, Spain, Italy, or some other European country to China? Do not introduce all that to them but only the faith."[36] Similarly, the eighteenth-century founder of the Holy Ghost Fathers made clear to prospective missionaries that they were not "going to Africa to establish there Italy or France or any such country. . . . Make yourselves Negroes with the Negroes. . . . Our holy religion has invariably to be established in the soil."[37]

This desire for people to receive the gospel in their heart language no doubt stood behind the Protestant Reformers' approach to Scripture as well. Luther utilized the new technology of the printing press and pioneered the principle of translating the Bible into the vernacular of the people. He was followed by reformers in other parts of Europe as well.[38] Calvin insisted that public prayers (like the Bible) should also be given in the language of the hearers, a radical move at the time.[39]

John and Charles Wesley famously adapted their approach to the culture of eighteenth-century Britain. They chose to "become more vile" by preaching in open-air settings, where the unchurched people were, and not just in the churches. Contextualization was also seen in the church music that they wrote, utilizing pub songs and other tunes common to the people they sought to reach.[40]

Hudson Taylor famously used these principles in his mission to China by adopting Chinese dress and customs. In a day when the approach to missions centered on the compound and colony, he at first earned himself the condemnation of his supporters in England, but they eventually recognized his approach as biblical.[41]

C. S. Lewis once suggested that part of a minister's ordination exam should be taking a passage from a theological text and translating it into everyday English. "It is absolutely disgraceful that we expect missionaries to the Bantus to learn Bantu, but never ask whether our missionaries to the Americans or English can speak American or English."[42]

EMBRACING THE BENEFITS AND AVOIDING THE DANGERS

Contextualization is not without its dangers, but neither is the failure to contextualize. Either accommodation to or isolation from the culture means God's mission goes unfulfilled. Lesslie Newbigin states brilliantly the tension missionaries live in:

On the one side there is the danger that one finds no point of

contact for the message as the missionary preaches it, to the
people of the local culture the message appears irrelevant
and meaningless. On the other side is the danger that the
point of contact determines entirely the way that the message is received, and the result is syncretism. Every missionary path has to find the way between these two dangers: ir-
relevance and syncretism. And if one is more afraid of one
danger than the other, one will certainly fall into the
opposite.[43]

Sometimes the case is made that attempts to change our approach do more harm than good. They end up reducing the challenge required by the gospel, diminishing the convert's opportunity to be discipled into the language of biblical Christianity or
deteriorating into nothing more than clever marketing, critics
say. These critiques have merit but should be taken as cautions on
how we contextualize, not as reasons to forgo contextualization
altogether.

We have to remember that even if we do not change our approach for the receiving culture, we are not necessarily presenting
a "purer" gospel or a gospel that is culture free. Rather, it is quite
possible that in not changing we are insisting that a person conform to cultural wrapping originally suited for another time and
place (presumably our own preferred time and place). We have
simply exchanged one set of cultural trappings for another. Or to
put it another way, if we choose not to adapt our forms to keep up
with a changing culture, at what point in the history of Christianity do we freeze ourselves culturally? Which of the many faithful
Christian traditions will we leave unaltered? Most often this question goes unasked. It is simply assumed that our way of communicating the gospel will be adequate for others.[44]

We would do better to present the message in a context suited
for the time and place we minister in. Erwin McManus puts it

well: "Many of our faith expressions are out of touch, not because they're ancient but because they're antiquated. . . . To become relevant is to catch up with the time in history you were intended to serve. Relevance is not about conformity; it is about clarity and connectedness."[45]

Rather than rejecting contextualization altogether, we must do our best to safeguard ourselves from the dangers of accommodation and syncretism. Noted missiologist Paul Hiebert advocates a four step safeguarding process, all of which apply in bringing the gospel to the post-Christian United States as well.[46] First, the missionaries must make a serious examination of the host culture.

Second, the pastor/missionary and subsequent church must exercise a strong commitment to biblical authority. Both the congregation and the pastor have crucial roles here. The church community itself must be immersed in the study of the Scriptures and growing in spiritual discernment. The pastor/missionary will be pivotal both for teaching the Bible in the new congregation and also in bringing the perspective of one who sees the Bible through different cultural lenses. The corporate dimension of this step allows the church to grow as a hermeneutical community, eventually providing its own checks and balances against syncretism.[47]

Third, the church must collectively evaluate their own past beliefs and customs in light of the biblical teaching, and discern how to handle the different aspects of their culture. The results of such an assessment will likely lead the church to keep some practices that are not unbiblical, reject some that are and modify others to give them Christian meaning. In addition, the new church will adopt rites drawn from common Christian practice (e.g., the Lord's Supper and baptism) and create new symbols and rituals which have particular meaning for them.[48]

Finally, the church will see itself as operating within a broad international network of churches. By paying attention to the church on a global level, they will be safeguarded from interpreting the Scriptures and practicing the faith in ways that are incompatible with an overarching Christian understanding.[49]

I would add to Hiebert's list (which is communal in nature) one further safeguard (which is more individual in nature). In 1 Corinthians 9, Paul's discussion moves naturally from his practice of contextualization (vv. 19-23) to his personal spiritual disciplines (vv. 24-27). This passage should not be taken as separate from the verses preceding it. For Paul to "become all things to all people" without slipping into sin or accommodation, he must beat his body and make it his slave. Embracing our call as God's missionary people requires that we face the spiritual dangers that come with this life. We cannot engage the culture and not be adversely affected by it unless we are grounded in God's Word, pursue a life characterized by the spiritual disciplines, and immerse ourselves in a vibrant church community.

CONCLUSION

As believers in Christ, we must embrace our vocation as God's missionary people. To do so faithfully will require us to become "bilingual," engaging in critical contextualization as we learn to proclaim our faith in the language of our hearers. This will involve a level of proficiency in cultural exegesis, as well as careful attention to the preservation of the message we carry. Contextualization follows the pattern of the incarnation, is demonstrated in the book of Acts, taught in the epistles and modeled throughout church history. This practice is crucial to our task of making disciples.

3

Living Out God's Mission in Disciplemaking

Then Jesus came to them and said, "All authority in heaven and on earth has been given to me. Therefore go and make disciples of all nations, baptizing them in the name of the Father and of the Son and of the Holy Spirit, and teaching them to obey everything I have commanded you. And surely I am with you always, to the very end of the age."

MATTHEW 28:18-20

It is not so much the case that God has a mission for his church in the world but that God has a church for his mission in the world. Mission was not made for the church; the church was made for mission—God's mission.

CHRISTOPHER J. H. WRIGHT,
THE MISSION OF GOD

My wife refers to Starbucks as "the office." I have an actual office, but typically at least half my work week takes place at one of my many "branch offices." I like the noise, and I like the people. Starbucks has an atmosphere that invites people to both do their own thing and interact with those around them, which makes it good for either study or meeting with others (and of course they have good coffee). But mostly I like it because it's one of our culture's

watering holes and a good place to make friends with people outside the church. I see my time at Starbucks as an important space
for me to live out Christ's command to make disciples.

Much has been written in recent years urging the church to
step away from a reduced view of the mission of God and to embrace a fuller biblical picture of God's work in the world. These are
reminders we need to hear. God is not interested solely in saving
souls but in restoring a broken world and the broken people who
inhabit it. He is concerned not just with people getting to heaven
when they die, but in seeing his kingdom come on earth and his
will done here as it is in heaven. The church has been rightly urged
to minister to people's physical as well as spiritual needs.

All of these things are true and need to be embraced as a cor-
rective to much of recent evangelicalism. God's mission of restoring our fallen world is one of cosmic proportions, and my intention here is not to reduce it in the least. Yet at the same time we
must be careful that in our efforts to be comprehensive we don't
lose sight of the simplicity of Christ's call, and of the individuals
he puts in our path. We dare not lose sight of the critical task of
evangelism or of the task of seeing those converts spiritually
formed into maturing apprentices of Jesus. In other words, we
mustn't loosen our grasp on Jesus' command to make disciples.

DISCIPLEMAKING: TWO APPROACHES
No definition of God's mission can be considered complete if it
does not take seriously the command of Jesus to make disciples.

Taking Matthew's Gospel as paradigmatic, the command to
make disciples is a broad one, carrying within it the picture of
what a disciple is and does, a commitment to live out the teachings of Jesus, the interconnectedness of Christ's disciples to one
another, and the calling to be those sent by God into the world.[1]
Those who make disciples are disciples themselves, learning what
it means to live as Jesus' apprentices. And the church exists as a

missionary community of these disciples, carrying out the Great Commission (Mt 28:18-20) as they live by the Great Commandment (Mt 22:37-40). Even when rightly seen in the larger context of God restoring a broken creation, the heart of God's mission is making people into Jesus' disciples.

This command to make disciples has been understood in different ways. Many understand it as evangelism. To them disciplemaking means converting people to saving faith in Jesus. Many others see mere evangelism as a shallow reading of the text and emphasize that these converts need to be discipled, which means attention must be given to the spiritual formation of believers. To them, what Jesus commanded was "discipleship," which generally involves some form of working through a curriculum to teach the basics of the faith.

Most of us, though, would agree that both evangelism and spiritual formation are part of the disciplemaking task. When Jesus says we are to baptize these disciples, we have to conclude that he is referring to those who have come to faith in him. When he tells us to teach these disciples to obey everything he has commanded, we conclude he is also referring to the ongoing spiritual growth of these converts.

A disciple is a Christian—not the supercharged version of a Christian, one that is more mature than "ordinary" Christians or one that has been through a certain curriculum.[2] A disciple is a person who has trusted in Jesus for salvation and consequently has enlisted as his apprentice, learning from him how to live, and becoming like him in the process. "Discipleship *is* the Christian life. And the goal of the Christian life is to become like Jesus."[3]

Seeing disciplemaking as falling primarily into one of these two categories (evangelism or spiritual formation) has introduced some unnecessary difficulties into the church's task. While these two activities are distinct, I think we would benefit from revisioning these in a more holistic way. Rather than viewing evangelism and spiritual formation as wholly separate tasks, we need to treat them as overlapping and interrelated aspects of a single task: disciplemaking.

Model 1. In the model I was trained in, evangelism was basically defined as everything that happens to lead a person toward Christ until that person becomes a Christian. Discipleship was defined as everything that happens to help a person grow in their faith after the person becomes a Christian. The two were totally separate. If I were to draw this model on the back of a napkin it would look like figure 3.1.

Figure 3.1. Model 1 of disciplemaking

The line on the left represents the process of evangelism, and the marks on the line represent different steps a person might take in coming to faith. In this model a Christian might meet a person, share the gospel with him or her, possibly bring the person to an outreach-oriented event and lead the person to the point of conversion.

The line on the right represents the process of discipleship. In this model a person would take a new believer through a follow-up process, introduce him or her to reading the Bible, prayer, attending a church and maybe a small group. This process continues in different forms throughout the believer's life as he or she grows in faith.

Between these two lines is a very important gap. Evangelism experts emphasize the importance of minimizing the gap between evangelism and discipleship by following up with the new believer as quickly as possible (many would say follow-up must begin within the first twenty-four hours). If the discipleship process does not begin right away, we risk seeing the new believer slip back into his or her former life and never become an active participant in the church.

This is the model I was taught, and which I became disillusioned with over time. Why was it that new believers were so prone to fall away if follow up was not immediate? Was conversion to Christ that fragile a thing? Why were new believers so resistant to follow-up? The most convicting question to me personally was, When had I ever challenged someone to count the cost of being Jesus' disciple? The answer was never. I was selling people a ticket to heaven, not a life of becoming like Jesus. No wonder they weren't returning my calls when I tried to follow-up so they could grow in their faith. That wasn't what they had signed up for, and they frankly had no interest in it. When I thought honestly about the results of this approach, I began to wonder how many "decisions" for Christ were not actual conversions but mere decisions—impulsive choices made in response to what looked like a pretty good deal.

Over time, I began to see that the model I was using was making it more difficult for people to live as actual disciples of Jesus. One of the difficulties stems from its overreliance on Paul's conversion as the normative biblical model for how conversion occurs. It does not take into account other biblical models, most notably the conversion of the twelve disciples. As a result, conversion is treated more as an event and less as a process.[4] For reasons to be discussed later, it is especially important with the postmodern generations to allow conversion to be a process.

A second difficulty is that the attrition rate under this model is notoriously high, and rarely are potential disciples truly challenged to consider what it will cost them to follow Jesus. In his excellent study on conversion, Richard Peace makes an interesting observation that encounter evangelism (sharing the gospel with a total stranger, who may or may not be at a place where they care to hear it) may actually serve to inoculate people against the gospel by offering them an inadequate experience of Jesus. In other words, this type of evangelism might do more to repel people than to draw them.[5] Anecdotally, it would seem this is especially true with the postmodern generation.

Dan Kimball refers to the postmodern generations as "post-Christian" because they have encountered some form of Christianity on a small scale (in a family member, as portrayed in religious programming, etc.), feel they now have an understanding of the faith and have already said "thanks but no thanks."[6] This is not to say that in a postmodern culture we will never utilize some form of encounter evangelism, but as we reach out to an increasingly post-Christian society an evangelism approach that fosters process will need to serve as our primary vehicle for outreach.

A third difficulty touches on issues of trust and assimilation into the church family. In this model new believers frequently feel as though they have been sold one thing, only to discover that they have bought another. Most respond to promises of eternal life and God's wonderful plan, only later to find out (in the follow-up process, if they make it that far) that growth in Christianity is also expected of them and that it involves all kinds of unappealing requirements: attending a church (irrelevant and boring), prayer (foreign), reading the Bible (difficult to understand), witnessing to others (scary), giving (you must be kidding) and more. These surprises frequently lead to disillusioned new believers who may or may not continue in the faith.

For those who do continue, growing into a mature and reproducing faith can be exceedingly difficult. The gospel presented to and accepted by them is essentially self-centered, and becoming other-centered often seems an intrusion rather than a normal part of Christian living. Their faith is seen as a personal matter, and the more rigorous demands of following Jesus, such as participating in a community of imperfect people, serving the needs of others, sharing the faith, and so forth, never become more than optional extras. In his study of conversion, Scot McKnight suggests that an overemphasis on personal decision can lead to a personal, and ultimately private, version of Christianity.[7] And as Dallas Willard says, if this is the Christianity that a person originally accepted, it is very difficult to "switch contracts" later on.

A fourth difficulty in this model is that since evangelism and discipleship are treated as completely separate activities, it feeds a pick-and-choose mentality among believers. Because most of what we do in the typical church is geared toward the spiritual growth of existing members, and because evangelism involves the discomfort of rejection, discipleship becomes the primary activity for believers. Evangelism is seen as optional; it rarely happens in the lives of most believers.

In fact, I would contend that one of the greatest barriers to evangelism is the sheer volume of activity we ask our congregants to participate in. We tell our people that we want them to build relationships with their non-Christian neighbors, but we also expect them to attend a small group, prayer meeting, special events we plan for them, serve in a ministry, protect their family time, have strong devotional habits, attend church on Sunday and so on. When is there any time left for building a friendship with anyone outside the church?

Model 2. I am suggesting we tweak the model, making the activities we normally associate with spiritual formation a larger part of our preconversion efforts as well.[8] A more holistic approach allows conversion to take place via a process rather than an event, and encourages potential disciples to see the Christian life up close and to count the cost of becoming a Christ follower. In employing many of the same ministry structures for believers and those investigating, we help believers make friendship with those who are far from God part of the normal Christian life rather than an optional extra. On my napkin this model would look like figure 3.2.

Evangelism and Spiritual Formation

Figure 3.2. Model 2 of disciplemaking

In this diagram there is only one line, representing both evangelism and spiritual formation. This model presupposes that more often than not conversion is a process, not a one-time encounter. Here, the believer comes alongside the non-Christian as a spiritual friend, and invites the friend's participation in a number of "Christian" activities, represented by the marks on the line. These might include any number of activities (a small group, worship gatherings, service events, social gatherings, etc.) depending on where the person is on their journey and which steps are most appropriate at any given time in helping him or her move toward a relationship with Christ. Those investigating the faith are invited into and embraced by the community of faith, allowing them to discover faith "from the inside," rather than having to make up their minds before really experiencing what the Christian life is like.

The dotted line in figure 3.2 represents the point of conversion. It is dotted not because the conversion is uncertain but because we may not be able to identify a day or hour when the person crossed over the line of faith and became a Christ follower. For many who come to faith in this way, the realization that they now believe and have become followers of Jesus comes gradually. The task of disciplemaking is happening on both sides of the dotted line, and often the activities we use to help make disciples look very similar from one side of conversion to the other.

As I read the Gospels, I see echoes of Jesus' approach in this model. In his ministry, Jesus proclaimed the gospel of the kingdom to committed followers and the crowds alike. Both the crowds and the committed experienced and witnessed the teaching, healing, and deliverance ministries of Jesus (see, for instance, the presence of both the disciples and the crowd in the Sermon on the Mount [Mt 5:1-2; 7:28; Lk 7:17-19]). Many in the crowd followed only for a short time, to investigate or to enjoy the benefits of healing and feeding (Jn 6:26), but many others at some point in the process became true believers (e.g., Nicodemus [Jn 3; 7:50; 19:39]). Jesus sums up this characteristic of his ministry in the parable of the soils (Mk 4:1-20).

Jesus seemed largely unconcerned with who was in and who was out ("You do not want to leave too, do you?" [Jn 6:67]), but simply called all to follow regardless of where they were at in the process, always inviting them to go deeper. This does not mean there wasn't deliberate preaching directed to the unconverted (e.g., Jn 4) and instruction on the spiritual life directed toward the already committed (e.g., Mk 9:2). Rather, Jesus' approach fostered a process that naturally included both aspects of disciplemaking: evangelism and formation.

It appears that a similar dynamic existed in the first-century church as well, because both believers and inquirers were present when the church gathered for worship. Paul urges the church to take care that their worship is understandable and beneficial to both groups (1 Cor 14:23-24). This was also true in the ancient church up through at least the fourth century. Seekers were invited to participate in a process of experience and investigation within the church community, which eventually brought them to conversion and to ongoing spiritual formation.[9]

My contention is that such an approach is biblically faithful, brings with it a number of benefits, and is especially suited for ministry in a postmodern context. This approach allows seekers to see and experience the Christian life before they commit to it. There is ample opportunity, not just to decide if Jesus is the truth but also to see what it means to be his disciple. This reduces the rate of attrition and the follow-up required for a new believer. In my experience the typical person coming to salvation by this approach has already been praying, reading the Bible and attending worship gatherings and a small group for at least three months before conversion. So in many ways follow-up is a nonissue. By intentionally shaping our ministry structures to be effective in both outreach and spiritual formation, evangelism is demarginalized and integrates more naturally into the everyday lives of believers. This approach also deals realistically with the limited amount of time that people with families and jobs have to invest in church-related activities.

Within this type of framework, what will our approaches to evangelism and spiritual formation look like? How will these practices change as we minister to those with a more postmodern worldview? The remainder of this chapter will examine shifts in our thinking that we need to make as we approach evangelism, and chapter four will examine shifts in our approach to spiritual formation.

Fruit Versus Roots

My friend Dave Olson is the director of church planting for the Evangelical Covenant Church, a role which has given him a front-row seat to the changes in our culture and in ministry over the past fifteen years. He describes the differences between evangelism in baby-boomer churches and in churches who are reaching out to postmoderns like this: evangelizing baby boomers is like picking fruit from an aging tree, while evangelizing postmoderns is like fertilizing the roots in hope that fruit will one day appear.

With the baby boomers (particularly between 1980 and 2000), ministry occurred in the midst of a secular culture that retained some religious memory. Enough of the trappings of Christendom remained that previous models could be tweaked and would still reach some people. The tree didn't have nearly as much fruit on it as it did in generations past, but it could be found if a person went to the right branches. Evangelism strategies revolved around find-ing the best ways to pick the fruit.

With postmoderns, ministry happens in a secular yet spiritu-ally curious context. Little religious memory is present; the church now functions on the margins and exists for most as a sort of cul-tural curiosity. Fruit is hard to find, and much of the work of evangelism is digging around the tree's roots and fertilizing. Strat-egies revolve around how to best cultivate the soil, while being attentive to the fruit that does appear on the tree.[10]

When I'm with leaders of emerging churches, I find reactions to the topic of evangelism very interesting. Some are embarrassed when the topic comes up (a reaction I know well) because they know the importance but aren't doing it very well or aren't seeing much in the way of results. I find others, though, who say things like, "We're not really about that," or "We're not too concerned with sharing the gospel, just living it." Still others say they value evangelism, but feel that to highlight the more neglected aspects of the gospel we must stop talking about (or at least greatly de-emphasize) evangelism.

I recognize the temptation here—the soil has gotten harder, and every conversion comes as the result of many hours of prayer and sweat. We know that the old strategies aren't working, but the new strategies have not yet matured, and there are few tools to replace those that have been set aside. What's more, as we redis-cover a more robust theology of the kingdom and a healthy long-ing for compassion and justice (practices for which results and gratification are immediate and tangible), it becomes more and more appealing to direct our outward-focused efforts toward these practices and to neglect evangelism.

Evangelism in this environment is hard—there are no two ways about it. But how can we claim to be faithful to the gospel without a theology that values conversion? While we should not reduce the message to this alone, it is undeniable that Jesus came to seek and save the lost. His church is tasked with the continuation of that rescue mission. This invitation to life in Christ is "the core, heart, or center of mission."[11] Scot McKnight issues a timely warning to the emerging church, pointing out that mainline church leaders in the early twentieth century never meant to abandon evangelism when they began to elevate the social aspects of the gospel. Yet that is exactly what happened.[12]

We cannot afford to be passive about reaching our generation. It is precisely because evangelism is so difficult in a postmodern world that Christian leaders must keep this value in front of our people. I'm struck whenever I read Paul's charge to Timothy, his gifted yet timid protégé: "Do the work of an evangelist," Paul reminds him (2 Tim 4:5). Similarly, as we discharge the duties of our ministries, we need to consistently teach God's heart for the lost and hurting, instruct our churches in evangelism in the best ways we know how and find ways to model it in our own lives.

SHIFTING FROM BASKETS TO SHOVELS

If more of our efforts are indeed directed at cultivating the soil, we need to rethink the tools needed for evangelism in the twenty-first century. As we do so, there are three broad shifts I suggest we make.

The first of these shifts is from evangelism as an event to evangelism as a process. Modern evangelistic efforts find their theological basis in Paul's conversion, as opposed to the conversion of the twelve disciples. Consequently, most of our tools are designed to create a mini-Damascus road event for a person: crusade evangelism, the altar call, sharing a tract with a person—all of which call a person to an on-the-spot decision for or against Christ. The proclamation of the message is itself considered the Damascus road experience. Though this approach is occasionally successful with those who have no Christian background, it is most effective with those who already hold some belief in Jesus and need to be called to commitment.

In contrast, postmodern people typically need more time. Their shallow prior experience with Christianity, distrust of the church as an institution, skepticism over truth claims and preference for religious pluralism make it very difficult to "manufacture" a Damascus road event. Furthermore, for the postmodern, truth is discerned primarily by experience. Of course Jesus will continue to meet some in a more dramatic fashion, but we should expect that most will be convinced of the reality of Christ over time. Evangelism as a process will be the norm.

As we grapple with this shift in the local church, we need to develop tools that do not discount Paul's experience, but which draw from the experience of the Twelve as well. We need to facilitate an evangelism process in which we allow people to walk with Jesus and his people over time, without the pressure to make up their minds during that one encounter.[13]

The second shift needed in twenty-first-century evangelism is from impersonal to personal. Most of the tools utilized in modern evangelism are essentially impersonal. The altar call, which has been popular in the United States since the mid-1800s, is a case in point.[14] The relationship between the preacher and the hearer is usually nonexistent. This is even less personal in settings where a person's conversion is completely anonymous. Sometimes those responding are told to pray and invite Jesus into their hearts while "every head is bowed and every eye is closed," making this an isolated decision in which even those sitting nearby are unaware that a decision for Christ may have occurred.

Crusade evangelism is also an impersonal exchange between a speaker and a stadium full of people. Likewise, I believe that much of the commonly practiced one-on-one evangelism, though occurring face to face, is impersonal. It often involves an encounter between a Christian with a tract and a total stranger. Little or no relationship exists beforehand, and ordinarily there is no relationship afterward (even if a person expresses a decision for Christ).

In contrast, it is very important in a postmodern setting for evangelism to be personal. Trust is not built in a vacuum but in relationship. Even though many find evangelism with strangers frightening, many more will admit it is more frightening with friends. It takes less emotional energy to risk rejection with someone you will never see again than it does to cultivate a real relationship with someone who does not know Christ. Doug Pagitt states it well: "People who can change our beliefs are people to whom we give the authority to suggest alternatives to us. It's hard to get around the idea of belief as a relational process."[15] Believers wanting to introduce Jesus to postmoderns will need to do the hard work of cultivating a relationship rather than hoping that a hit-and-run approach will be enough.

The third shift is from a rational to an embodied apologetic. Rational apologetics will continue to be an important tool, but an embodied apologetic will be the first foot forward in convincing postmoderns of the truth of the faith.

In suggesting these shifts, I want to be careful not to appear overly critical of any of the evangelistic tools mentioned previously. Countless people have found Christ as a result of these, and they offer much to commend. These approaches should be commended first for their intentionality, which the emerging church often lacks. In struggling with how to approach a shifting culture, emerging churches often fail to practice evangelism at all. Also, many of these approaches are good examples of contextualization. They were well-suited to their time and cultural circumstances, even if they aren't well-suited for a postmodern mission field. Door-to-door evangelism, for instance, made sense in a time when people opened their doors to buy vacuums, encyclopedias and hair brushes. Currently this approach has largely been abandoned, even by modern churches, as so few people appreciate salespeople coming to their door.

These approaches do, however, bring certain theological implications we need to keep in mind as we evaluate them, and as we develop new tools as well. Evangelistic methods that are event-oriented, impersonal and more rational than embodied contribute to the bracketing off of evangelism from the rest of a Christian's life. In addition, such an approach virtually invites nonparticipation at a church level in the life of a new convert. It should come as no surprise that evangelism this removed from the church results in very high attrition rates. In addition, these approaches should also raise some concern in terms of the authenticity of the resulting conversions. Have those who prayed a "sinner's prayer" actually come into a saving relationship with Jesus? Is there saving faith behind the prayer or are they merely mouthing words? We need to be reminded that it is faith that saves us, not the words a person recites. Too often we treat such a prayer as a defining test of salvation, rather than looking at the fruits that come with repentance. Borrowing the words of Jesus in the parable of the soils, we must be careful that we do not rush to assure a person of the efficacy of his or her conversion when the seeds may in fact have fallen on the path or on rocky or thorny soil. Time and the resulting fruit will tell if the conversion is real or not.

FIRST-CENTURY EVANGELISM IN THE TWENTY-FIRST CENTURY

I want to close this chapter with one final passage from the ministry of Paul that I find especially helpful as we consider making disciples in our increasingly post-Christian mission field. The church in Colosse was started as a result of the church planting movement ignited in Ephesus, where, Luke tells us, the gospel spread so rapidly that in two years' time "all the Jews and Greeks who lived in the province of Asia [Minor] heard the word of the Lord" (Acts 19:10). In the conclusion to his letter to the Colossian believers, Paul reminds them of their vocation as God's missionary people and instructs them as they continue in the work of the gospel in their context.

Pray. "Devote yourselves to prayer, being watchful and thankful," Paul says. "And pray for us, too, that God may open a door for our message, so that we may proclaim the mystery of Christ, for which I am in chains. Pray that I may proclaim it clearly, as I should" (Col 4:2-4).

Paul begins his exhortation to this young church with a reminder to rely on God's power, not their own. The difficulty of ministry in a culture without Christian roots serves as a vivid reminder that salvation is a supernatural event, and only God can bring it about. This is a value that he models even as he asks them to pray for him as well. Such evangelistic prayer has several distinct qualities.

First, it is constant. Paul calls the Colossians to *devote* themselves to prayer. This is not a passing activity but ongoing labor on behalf of those lost people that God puts in our lives. As Oswald Chambers wrote, "Prayer does not equip us for greater works—prayer *is* the greater work."[16] If we are to see God's work in people's lives, we need to be diligent in our prayer for them.

Second, such prayer is attentive to what God is doing. Paul tells these believers to be "watchful and thankful" as they pray. Throughout the book of Acts, Luke reports how in every new city Paul is able to seek out those people who are open to the gospel, and these people form the core of each new church plant. Paul operates with an understanding that God is at work, and we need to have our eyes open to see in whom God is doing his work. And Paul does so in a spirit of gratitude, rejoicing even in the face of tremendous suffering as God's work goes forward.

This same dynamic can be seen in the instructions Jesus gave the seventy-two as he sent them out into towns where Jesus had not yet gone. He instructed them to first offer a blessing when they came to a house, and if "the head of the house loves peace," they were to stay there and proclaim and demonstrate the reality of the kingdom (Lk 10:5-11).

Third, and related to this attentiveness, Paul prays that God will open doors for their message. He asks God to go ahead of them, preparing hearts and creating opportunities for them to speak (cf. Jn 6:44). Finally, Paul prays that when the opportunities do come, that he will be faithful with the message, proclaiming the mystery of the gospel clearly.

As Starbucks has become my unofficial office, it has become my habit to silently pray for the crew members and regular customers as I work. I pray for God's blessing on them, and pray that God will draw them to himself. Many of these people have become friends, and it is amazing to watch how over time people's hearts soften toward me and then toward God. Over time I've found that I'm better off not sharing the gospel until I've spent a lot of time praying that a door will open for the message. When I'm faithful to pray, more often than not I find out the door has popped open because my friend will suddenly approach me and start asking questions about God.

For a long time I prayed that God would draw to himself a young barista named Kelly. One morning as I was ordering my coffee she blurted out, "I'm breaking up with my boyfriend tonight!" I looked behind me to see who she was talking to, but sure enough it was me! I listened as she shared the reasons she felt she needed to do this, and her growing recognition that God wanted her out of this unhealthy relationship. I said, "Thanks for sharing that with me, Kelly—I'll be praying for you tonight." She sighed a grateful thank you and moved on to the growing line of customers behind me. The next day during her break I asked how it went, and a spiritual friendship began. We talked all about the God who made her and loves her, and cares deeply that she finds love with a man who would treat her as she deserves. I and others in our faith community had the privilege of walking with her as she rediscovered her faith and as God brought deep healing in her life. Now she is part of our leadership and shepherds one of our ministry teams.

I prayed for a long time for another young woman at Starbucks, a single mom who was working her way through school. I was disappointed when she transferred to another location before a spiritual friendship could develop between us, but was thrilled two years later to be greeted by her when I was visiting one of our congregation's church plants! Unbeknownst to me, God had been working in her heart, and through a whole different web of relationships she ended up following Jesus as part of our daughter congregation.

I find it significant that more than half of Paul's instructions in this passage are about how to pray, because I've come to believe that the bulk of the work of evangelism is prayer. Salvation is the work of God, and his work of evangelism always precedes ours.

Act. "Be wise in the way you act toward outsiders; make the most of every opportunity" (Col 4:5). Second, Paul reminds the Colossians that their actions will be an important part of their witness to those around them. This gets to the heart of the embodied apologetic we are discussing: as others experience God in our midst, see the quality of love lived out in our community and see the practical enacting of our faith bringing good to the surrounding world, our faith becomes more real to them.

Last night after worship I talked to a young woman who had detoured from her faith some years back (one of the many dechurched people God loves to bring us). I had seen her while I was giving the message and could see in her face that she was really being affected. I saw her again as we worshiped and took communion, and by this point she was sobbing. After the service we were talking, and when we were out of the hearing of others she said, "I want to tell you what brought me here. My friend James has been inviting me to this church for about a year, and he told me he was speaking tonight." James is a young man in our church who is gay and is struggling with the realities of living faithfully as a follower of Jesus. He has been wonderfully open with our church about how tough the battle has been and the wins and losses he's experienced in leading a celibate life. "That's great you came out to support him," I replied. "It's more than that," she said as tears again filled her eyes. "I know a lot of Christians, but the only person who consistently invites me to church is my gay friend. He loves it here and always talks about the grace he is experiencing. And I just had to know—what kind of church is this that my *gay* friend can feel so accepted in and be so excited about?" For her and many others that have found their way to Life Covenant Church, it was the actions and attitude of the community, displayed and relayed through a friend, that led them to consider Christ.

Speak. Finally, Paul instructs the Colossians on the posture of their verbal witness. "Let your conversation be always full of grace, seasoned with salt, so that you may know how to answer everyone" (Col 4:6). Much of modern evangelism and apologetics tends to have a combative, pushy tone, reminiscent of a formal debate on the one hand or an aggressive sales pitch on the other ("apologetics as martial arts," as one commentator has described it).[17] Contrary to this, Paul calls the Colossian believers to speech that is graceful and winsome.

Two expressions he uses imply that there is something in the way we speak that should cause people to want more. "Seasoned with salt" would imply that the conversation has an appealing, flavorful and perhaps thirst-inducing quality to it. That believers would need to "answer" others implies that someone is raising a question.

In an incarnational approach to ministry, there is a temptation to pull back at the point of verbal witness. Faithful prayer and wise action have broken up the soil, and the ground is ready to receive seed. But the fact is, if we never actually sow, there will be no harvest. Action alone is insufficient—at the proper time a verbal witness is essential.

Because I spend so much time at Starbucks, a good number of the stories I tell about God's work are set there. A while back I received an encouraging e-mail from a member of our church who was reflecting on some stories I had shared that night in the message. Here is part of what she wrote:

> For a while, I was thinking, well [he has these stories] because he is a pastor and that's what he does every day. While that is true, it also reminds me that I am called to the same thing. I have similar opportunities to talk with and pray for the people I work with all day. And I have no excuse not to do it. I really want to pursue that and use my workplace as my own "Starbucks."

Conclusion

At the heart of Christian mission is the ministry of disciplemaking. As we consider this mandate in our twenty-first-century context, we will benefit from approaching the task holistically, treating evangelism and spiritual formation as overlapping and interrelated activities rather than as wholly separate ones.

This will involve shifts in the way we approach evangelism, as well as in the way we approach spiritual formation.

4

Disciplines of Disciples

As the Father has sent me, so I send you.

JOHN 20:21 NRSV

Church people think about how to get people into the church;
kingdom people think about how to get the church into the world.
Church people worry that the world might change the church;
kingdom people work to see the church change the world.

HOWARD SNYDER, *LIBERATING THE CHURCH*

Our church was about five minutes old when we first began talking about starting more churches. From day one our congregation has shared this crazy dream, passion, burden and prayer that God would somehow use us (along with the churches we start) in planting a thousand churches in the United States and eventually all over the world. That first day in our living room we set a prayerful goal of planting a second church in our first few years together, and then to attempt to start one church every year after that. So far we've been deeply blessed to plant two more churches, and as I write this we are taking steps toward planting a third church.

When we committed to planting more churches, I had in mind the mission field—the thousands of young adults who simply won't be reached by more established churches, and who need churches that are unafraid to embrace the twenty-first-century mission field.[1] What I didn't expect was just how great an impact church planting would have on our church's spiritual formation. Planting new churches has turned out to be one of the most dynamic sources of spiritual growth at Life Covenant.

When we planted our first church it was a real step of faith. Doug was a gifted young pastor who came on our staff as our "church planter in residence," and spent a year being immersed in every aspect of church-planting life—from vision and preaching to children's ministry, budgets and church discipline. At the end of that time we raised money to send him out. We plant in partnership with our denomination, and Life's portion of the financial commitment to this new plant was $40,000 over three years.

This was a big reach for us. We are a small congregation, 80 percent of whom are in their twenties and thirties. What's more, as our leadership prayed we felt called to ask our church to raise the money all at once rather than over three years, so we would be free to continue planting without worrying about completing our commitment to earlier churches. To our utter amazement and joy, the money was raised in six weeks! Twelve months later we planted our second church, and issued the same challenge to the church to raise the money all at once. This time the money came in only three weeks.

Our church is not wealthy. To give this much above our regular budget means people had to stretch, sacrifice, pray, rethink family budgets, sell things. And I kid you not, as people wrote their checks, they were asking me, "We're doing this again next year, right?"

Mission is for the good of the world, but also works for the good of God's people. It is central to how God forms us as disciples of Jesus. "I pray that you may be active in sharing your faith," Paul writes to Philemon, "so that you will have a full understanding of every good thing we have in Christ" (Philem 6 NIV). The fuller life in Christ comes not only as we give attention to our own growth but largely as we give ourselves away. And Paul reminds the church in Ephesus that growth in faith, knowledge, maturity and unity will come as God's people are equipped to serve others (Eph 4:11-16).

GOING INWARD TO GO OUTWARD

Much of the church's approach to spiritual formation rightly focuses on the inner life, but if this is not paired with a robust outward focus it can lead to imbalance. It is ironic, but helping people grow in Christ can become an impediment to mission. When our own positive experiences of encountering God in worship and devotion are especially satisfying, it can be difficult "to return to the valleys of men, where there are demons to be cast out."[2] Peter and the disciples on the Mount of Transfiguration were ready to linger in the divine presence as long as possible. What a shocking contrast to come off the mountain and reenter a world convulsing, screaming, and foaming at the mouth, where disciples valiantly strive to do the work of God as disgruntled critics complain about the service they are receiving (Lk 9:28-45). Ministry is messy, evangelism can be painful and, as the disciples discovered, living out the mission of God can lead to major headaches. At times we are our own worst enemies, preferring to meet God exclusively on the mountain and avoid him in the trenches.

Yet that fuller experience of God we look for is not found in attempts to perpetually remain on the mountaintop. Rather, we find our greatest satisfaction in God as we follow him into the messiness of the valley. Twentieth-century mystic Thomas Kelly writes about the Christian's paradoxical relationship with the world: "He plucks the world out of our hearts, loosening the chains of attachment. And He hurls the world into our hearts, where we and He together carry it in infinitely tender love."[3] We encounter God's heart most deeply as his love sends us out into the world.

When the mission degenerates into serving ourselves, we not only fail to live out God's mission but miss much of the rich formation God would birth in us as a result. Theologian Ray S. Anderson tells us that, more than ministry to those within the church, it is mission to those outside the church that brings the spiritual vitality the church desires. "[Outward-focused] mission, rather than [inward-directed] ministry, expands God's kingdom and renews the spiritual life of the church. Ministry expends Spirit in programs and body building; mission breathes in Spirit and promotes body movement."[4]

This outward dimension of spiritual formation in no way takes away from the inner life. On the contrary, cultivating rich devotional practices is critical. But if inner growth is not directed toward outward movement, the result is believers whose growth is stunted.

DISCIPLEMAKING: SPIRITUAL FORMATION AS APPRENTICESHIP TO JESUS

God wants to change us. His goal is to make us like Jesus—to conform us to the image of his Son (Rom 8:29). When we speak of being and making disciples, we always have in mind that by God's grace we are transformed, not just forgiven of our sins. To this end, God will never be satisfied with a superficial change in our behavior, but only with heart-level transformation. He wants to make us the type of people who naturally do the things that Jesus did, and who will be fit to reign with him in eternity.

Dallas Willard's articulation of spiritual formation has been instrumental for our church. He says, "Spiritual formation for the Christian basically refers to the Spirit-driven process of forming the inner world of the human self in such a way that it becomes like the inner being of Christ himself."[5]

This kind of spiritual change does not happen automatically. All spiritual growth comes as a result of God's work in our lives, but we are not merely passive recipients in this process. God initiates but then invites our participation in the process of spiritual formation and transformation into Christlikeness. Willard says,

> If we—through well-directed and unrelenting action— effectually receive the grace of God in salvation and transformation, we certainly will be incrementally changed toward inward Christlikeness. The transformation of the outer life, especially of our behavior, will follow suit.[6]

God works in conjunction with our actions, working change in our character through his grace. As a result, our action makes a tremendous difference in the way we grow as Christians.

According to Willard, three elements are necessary for lasting spiritual change to occur. In what he calls the "reliable pattern" of personal transformation, a person must have a *vision* for what he or she can become, the *intention* to work toward the accomplishment of this vision and the *means* to fulfill that vision.[7] Too often we tell people to go and do (means) without any real vision of what the result should be, or we inspire (vision) but give them no plan, or we give these other components but fail to nurture intent. The church must foster all three of these elements in order to help its people toward genuine transformation.

Vision. If we hope to see genuine transformation in our lives, it is important that we believe it can actually happen and that we have some idea of what that transformation will look like. As I pursue my own spiritual formation and that of those I lead, two key words from Scripture help enlarge my vision of what life in Jesus might look like: *becoming* and *kingdom*.

Scripture describes salvation not just as the forgiveness of sin but as a process of becoming like Jesus. Everyone who has received salvation from God is in the process of being transformed into the likeness of Christ.

The promises of Scripture to believers are unblushing in their scope and would strike our ears as blasphemous if they didn't come from God himself. As we reflect the Lord's glory in our lives, Paul says, we are actually "being transformed into his image" (2 Cor 3:18). In Romans Paul declares that it is God's unshakeable intention that all who believe will be conformed to the likeness of Jesus (Rom 8:29). Elsewhere, Paul describes his pastoral work as seeing that "Christ is formed" in believers (Gal 4:19). Similarly, Peter tells us that we actually "participate in the divine nature" (2 Pet 1:4), and John writes that as children of God our true selves are not yet seen, but that when Christ appears "we shall be like him" (1 Jn 3:2). "For you died," Paul writes, "and your life is now hidden with Christ in God. When Christ, who is your life, appears, then you also will appear with him in glory" (Col 3:3-4).

The great spiritual writers throughout church history give us an array of depictions of what this becoming like Christ might look like. To read the humble intimacy Thomas à Kempis modeled ("Oh my God and my All! What more can I possess? What greater joy can I desire?"),[8] the simplicity and joy of relationship we see in Brother Lawrence, who found God as readily in washing dishes as he did in retreats into solitude,[9] the peace amid trials and sheer joy of experiencing God that Madame Guyon's life exemplifies— these and more provide a compelling vision of what life in the Spirit can be like.[10]

The second word that I find enlarges my vision of following Jesus is *kingdom*. Jesus came preaching that the kingdom of heaven has come (Mt 4:17; Mk 1:15; Lk 4:43). The bulk of his parables and other teaching have to do with the nature of the kingdom of God (or kingdom of heaven, in Matthew's Gospel) and how we are to live in this kingdom. In spite of this, the kingdom gets little attention in our churches. In my own life as a Christian, I cannot remember hearing a single sermon on the kingdom of God, and it has only been in the last few years that I have begun to grapple with the question of what Jesus meant by the kingdom.

The kingdom of God is where God's will is done. It is "the range of his effective will" or rule, and within this domain what God desires for his world comes to pass.[11] This world was originally created by God as a place of beauty and perfection, where we would live in relationship with God and reign with him forever. But now the world is fallen, stained by sin and filled with disease, suffering, tragedy, and death. God's will is no longer done here the way that it is in heaven, and our role of reigning with God in this world has been disrupted. The Bible is the story of God restoring his rule. His kingdom rule is extended through the earth until Christ's return, when that rule will be made complete. In our church, we like to say that the kingdom of God is "the place where things happen like they should."

The gospel Jesus announced, demonstrated and taught was that God's kingdom is available, and we have the opportunity to live in and experience it *now*. This comes as we place our trust in Jesus and determine to live as his apprentices. The kingdom is breaking in, and as Christ's disciples we participate in extending God's kingdom rule to the ends of the earth. Like beams of light breaking through the cracked boards in a dark shed, God's rule is breaking into human history, increasingly filling the world with light until its completion at the return of Christ. And the church serves as the world's first taste of this kingdom, and as God's instrument in advancing his reign throughout the earth.[12]

When our vision of being disciples of Jesus involves living as kingdom people, we find ourselves thrust into both the inward and outward dimensions of spiritual formation. Our inner life— thoughts, attitudes, desires, reactions—become more and more like those of Jesus. And the fruit is that the world starts looking more like God reigns here. As we measure our growth in Christ, we need to ask ourselves this kingdom question: In my sphere of influence are things happening like they should?

To grow deep in Christ we must have a vision of what life in the kingdom is like and of actually becoming like Christ. First, we must believe that it is possible. Then we must understand the process for getting there. C. S. Lewis was certainly right when he wrote,

> Our Lord finds our desires not too strong, but too weak. We are half-hearted creatures, fooling about with drink and sex and ambition when infinite joy is offered to us, like an ignorant child who wants to go on making mud pies in a slum because he cannot imagine what is meant by the offer of a holiday at the sea. We are far too easily pleased.[13]

In other words, our vision is too small. Without a clear, compelling and oft-repeated vision of the glory that Christ offers, we will not be compelled to pursue Christlikeness.

Intention. Even as we hold in front of ourselves a vision of what the disciple's life can be, we need to nurture the intent to live this kingdom life and to grow into Christlikeness. We must make a decision to apprentice ourselves to Jesus, learn from him, trust him and obey his teachings. Without such a decision, our growth sputters and we drift through life in a fog of spiritual mediocrity.

Jesus speaks directly to the issue of intent when he boldly states that his followers teach his disciples "to obey everything I have commanded" (Mt 28:20). Our relationship with God must move beyond holding beliefs about Jesus to trusting Jesus in the way we live our daily lives. In practical terms this means obedience. If Jesus is who he said he is, then such teachings as the Sermon on the Mount, which on the surface seem unrealistic, are the wisest possible instructions on how to live.[14] Indeed, for Jesus and his hearers (unlike the ancient Greeks, and us as their descendants), teaching is more than an intellectual activity. "Jesus' teaching is an appeal to his listeners' will, not primarily to their intellect; it is a call for a concrete decision to follow him and submit to God's will."[15] The person who trusts Jesus will obey his teachings. Obedience is the evidence of the life that trusts (Jn 14:23).

Paul's clear intention to live like Jesus is unmistakable: "I do not run like someone running aimlessly; I do not fight like a boxer beating the air. No, I strike a blow to my body and make it my slave so that after I have preached to others, I myself will not be disqualified for the prize" (1 Cor 9:26-27). William Law stands out as a spiritual writer who saw clearly and passionately that we need to be intentional if we are to live like Jesus. His comments go straight to the heart:

> You see two persons: one is regularly in public and private prayer, the other is not. Now the reason for this difference is not this, that one has strength and power to observe prayer, and the other has not; but the reason is this, that one *intends* to please God in the duties of devotion, and the other *has no intention* about it.[16]

For many believers this is the part of the process where spiritual formation breaks down. Too often we present the gospel as a set of truths we must subscribe to, as opposed to a relationship with Jesus. Rather than calling people to put their trust in Jesus and become his follower, we simply ask them to believe certain truths. As a result, we see people who profess a decision for Christ but have no idea of what it means to actually be his disciple, and little concept that they will be changed by him. There is no intent to become like Christ because the opportunity they were presented simply offered a promise of heaven in exchange for a prayer requesting forgiveness.[17]

For others, there is a vague wish to become more like Jesus, but this never manifests itself in action. If they were completely honest, even if presented with a plan for becoming Christlike, they would have to say that they simply do not want to change (or at least do not want to change if it involves effort on their part).

In the church we nurture intent as we present a compelling vision of the discipled life, offer clear means by which people can move into this vision, and urge and model doing and not merely hearing the Word. Yet vision and intention alone are not enough. Scripture and the witness of the great men and women of the church tell us that we must pursue a method or means of formation if we are to experience rich growth in Christ.

Means. If we are fueled by a vision of becoming like Jesus, and if we truly intend to see this happen, then we must apply ourselves to the pursuit of this goal. This will necessarily involve the use of certain means to achieve the end that we desire. Spiritual formation is methodical. In the local church, everyone should be prepared to answer the question, What am I doing to be formed into Christ's image?

Simply trying harder to do the things Jesus did or to avoid the things that Jesus avoided will not be enough. As Paul told his young protégé, we have to *train* ourselves to be godly (1 Tim 4:8).

A few years ago I went to cheer on a friend as she ran a marathon. I've always hated running, but as I sat there watching all those people cross the finish line I couldn't help but wonder if I was capable of something like that. The next day I went out and ran a few very painful miles. I did it again the next few days, and a week later found that I could add one more mile to my run without collapsing. Before long I started wondering if I could work my way up to a 10K. As time went by I came to really love my runs (especially since I found that my best praying happens when I run), and eventually I committed to a year-long training regimen for a marathon.

Training is different than trying. If I had gone out that first day and attempted to run twenty-six miles, I would have collapsed in a heap by mile five. Even if I tried as hard as I possibly could, my body would not have been able to do what my mind commanded it to do. But a process of training allowed me to grow incrementally stronger until the impossible became possible. Training allows us to do things that we cannot do simply by trying.[18]

In the spiritual life, Richard Foster refers to this as the principle of "indirection."[19] We cannot become godly people as a result of direct effort. Rather, we direct our efforts toward leaning into Jesus and his work in us, and allowing him to shape our heart, soul, mind and strength toward him. In doing this (which is something we can do) we receive power from God to pray for our enemies, bless those who curse us, forgive others their debts, not be proud or judgmental and so on (things we cannot presently do). This is no doubt the kind of thing Paul had in mind when he said that those who "live by the Spirit" would not gratify the desires of their sinful nature. If one is walking closely with God, our inner life, including our desires, begins to change. And the end result is nothing less than love, joy, peace, patience, kindness, goodness, faithfulness, gentleness and self-control (Gal 5:16, 22-23). In other words, it is a life that looks like Jesus.

This is where the spiritual disciplines come in. A spiritual discipline is any practice that enables a person to do through training what he or she is not able to do simply by trying.[20] They are the practices, relationships and experiences that bring our minds and bodies into cooperation with God's work in our lives, making us more capable of receiving more of his life and power.

There is great variety to the means we can use, just as there are a potentially endless number of practices that can serve as spiritual disciplines. There are a number of classic spiritual disciplines, though, that have been practiced by God's people over the centuries. Richard Foster's seminal work on the disciplines lists twelve: meditation, prayer, fasting, study, simplicity, solitude, submission, service, confession, worship, guidance and celebration.[21] To this list of classic disciplines we could add praying the Psalms, practicing the presence of God, hesychastic or "breath" prayers, the daily examen, spiritual direction, the discipline of secrecy, fellowship and others.[22]

Sometimes people resist the spiritual disciplines, mistakenly thinking that they look to our own human effort to change us. But this is a misunderstanding of what spiritual disciplines are meant to achieve. Simply increasing our willpower or becoming more self-disciplined will not make us holy. Spiritual formation is a matter of our behavior flowing out of a transformed heart ("Good people bring good things out of the good stored up in their heart" [Lk 6:45]). Temptation is not adequately resisted, nor is virtue attained simply through willpower, but through allowing the Spirit of God to fill, direct and transform our lives (Rom 12:1-2; Gal 5:16-23; Col 2:20–3:5). When we practice the spiritual disciplines, we yield ourselves to God and make ourselves pliable for his work in our lives (see Rom 6:13). We involve our minds and bodies in the pursuit of holiness by putting ourselves in a position for God to work in us. As modern mystic Frank Laubach put it, "I have done nothing but open windows—God has done all the rest,"[23] and Richard Foster reminds us, "The path does not produce the change; it only places us where the change can occur."[24]

The necessity of employing means in order to mature spiritually has long been attested to by spiritual masters throughout the church's history. In addition to the testimony of Scripture, the spiritual masters of every age recognized the importance of the spiritual disciplines for spiritual growth. The desert fathers have long been revered for their intense pursuit of solitude, silence and simplicity as a means of intimacy with God. These men and women sought the desert as "the furnace of transformation," in which their lives would be purified.[25]

Beginning with Augustine, monastic communities established a pattern of life called a "rule" to ensure that life together would result in the deliberate spiritual formation of the monks.[26] The rule was not seen as a burden or a harsh means of dealing with oneself, but as "an instrument for shaping a particular kind of life for which a person has deep and genuine desire."[27] For centuries religious communities were built around these rules as a definite means of growing spiritually. In later years the mendicant orders shifted the focus of the rule of life to include more outward focused activities as well as contemplative ones. For the Franciscans and Dominicans it became increasingly clear that the prayer-filled life must overflow in outer action, and preaching the gospel and care for the poor became hallmarks of these traditions.[28]

One of the more rigorous uses of means for attaining spiritual growth comes from Ignatius of Loyola, whose intense spiritual exercises shaped Catholic spirituality for centuries.[29] In Protestantism as well, means were recognized as necessary for spiritual growth and were key to the spirituality of the Reformers and their successors. Luther took very seriously the spiritual disciplines in his own growth.[30] Calvin did as well, and cited faithful prayer as a key instrument for "penetrating to those riches which are treasured up for us with our heavenly Father."[31] In his very practical seventeenth-century classic, Jeremy Taylor suggests all manner of spiritual disciplines for growth in holiness in every aspect of life—public and private, secular and religious.[32]

Teaching people to follow a rule of life has been a valuable tool at Life. During our annual spiritual disciplines seminar/retreat, we give people time to prayerfully map out a plan for their spiritual formation that includes different disciplines, physical exercise, time with family and the like. Mapping out the means we will employ in pursuing our apprenticeship to Jesus keeps us from being haphazard in our approach to formation.[33] It reminds us that though spiritual growth comes from God's hand, it is not automatic but rather happens as we employ appropriate means.

Is It Working?

How do we measure whether spiritual formation is actually happening in the lives of our church members? Often spiritual growth is measured by the amount of time or effort put into certain spiritual practices (most frequently church attendance and daily quiet times). As important as these and other practices are for our spiritual growth, the more important question is whether we are letting God use these practices to transform us. The Pharisees were very disciplined Bible students, meticulous tithers and faithful worship attendees, but in spite of this they were becoming less, not more, spiritually mature, and growing further away from God (Mt 23; Jn 5:39-40).

Jesus said that the Law and Prophets were summed up in the command to love God with our entire beings and to love our neighbor as we love ourselves. Am I engaged in the spiritual disciplines? is an important question to ask, but an even more telling question is, Am I growing in love with God and with people?[34] In addition to considering whether we know more of the Scriptures today than we did a year ago, we need to consider whether we are kinder than we were a year ago, whether we sacrifice more readily for others, if we are growing less selfish, craving recognition less, becoming more truthful. It is in our ordinary, everyday behavior that we will see whether or not the disciplines are having an effect on us. William Law states it powerfully, "If we are to follow Christ, it must be in our common way of spending every day. Thus it is in all the virtues and holy tempers of Christianity; they are not ours unless they be the virtues and tempers of our *ordinary life*."[35]

At the same time that we lead others into a life of practicing the spiritual disciplines (and as we ourselves practice them) we must be careful that we do so in a way that helps them avoid making the disciplines an end in themselves. There is a very real danger that the disciplines degenerate into nothing more than a daily activity that we check off of our list of things to do. They can easily become "boundary markers" by which we judge our own spirituality and that of others. This can lead to a very dangerous state of "pseudotransformation," in which we have picked up the right things to say and do, but they do not flow from a renewed heart.

In that state, we look and sound like transformed people, but in reality we are not.[36]

There are two errors we commonly make in the practice of spiritual disciplines that hinder our growth into Christlikeness. The first is to neglect the disciplines altogether because we believe that spiritual growth will happen on its own. Sometimes this resistance comes from the well-intentioned (yet incorrect) belief that working to grow spiritually is somehow equivalent to working for our salvation. We are saved entirely through grace, and it is also by God's grace and initiative that we continue to grow and mature as Christians. This does not, however, relieve us of the responsibility to actively participate in the work God desires to accomplish in us and through us. As Willard says, "Grace is not opposed to effort, but to earning."[37] An incomplete understanding of grace perpetuates this, as we tend to connect grace exclusively with the forgiveness of sins, and not with Christ's empowerment to live the spiritual life. The greater the pursuit of holiness, the more grace we need.

The other error we commonly fall into in the pursuit of spiritual disciplines is the tendency to turn the spiritual disciplines into laws.[38] The disciplines are meant to be a blessing that brings freedom, but they can degenerate into a curse that enslaves us. There is a danger that they will become just another external marker rather than the means for transformation they are meant to be. We must avoid the temptation to measure our spiritual maturity merely by the practice of the disciplines themselves rather than by the fruit that they produce in our lives.

CHANGING OUR POSTURE

Too often our posture has been wrong in disciplemaking. Even when the substance was right, the posture or attitude has at times conveyed a poorer picture of the Jesus way of life than we would hope. Evangelism on the one hand looked like marketing Jesus, complete with slick sales pitches and clever slogans, or it has looked like pushy and combative debate, complete with logical traps for our opponent. Spiritual formation too has taken improper postures at times, with formulaic plans for growth, an overemphasis on acquiring knowledge and an overbearing authority on the part of those doing the "discipling."

These postures find a deeply held resistance in postmodern hearers and add to the perception that the church is plastic, offering little in the way of actual spirituality. This is a resistance that we should appreciate, as it moves us toward postures that are not only pragmatic but biblical. As this chapter concludes, I offer several suggestions on attitudes and practices that we need to cultivate as we make disciples of postmodern people.

Authenticity. Os Guinness relates a story of a Japanese businessman who describes the difference he sees between Christians and members of other faiths: "Whenever I meet a Buddhist leader, I meet a holy man. Whenever I meet a Christian leader, I meet a manager."[39] In our daily lives and in our presentation of the gospel, we must be authentic if we hope to be heard.

Postmodern people, skeptical as they are of the church, have an innate ability to sniff out phoniness. This will require us to be open and honest about our failures, and humble about our successes. It will require us to avoid sugarcoating, and to speak plainly about our beliefs and our stance on issues.

Humility. The posture of the Christian in postmodernity must be that of a "fellow traveler," not of one who has already arrived or who has all the answers. In a world that is hypersensitive to intolerance and to claims of absolute truth, truth must be presented, but with special care given to gentleness, humility and a genuine open-mindedness.

Two aspects of Paul's approach in Athens (see chap. 3) seem well-suited for this. One way we display humility is by remembering that God has been working in a person's life before we arrived as a messenger. Jesus taught that no one comes to him without the Father's drawing that person (Jn 6:44), and we trust that the drawing process is already in motion. In recognizing that we are joining God in the work he is already doing in our friends' lives, we avoid the appearance of arrogance that so often accompanies evangelism.[40]

A second practice is by arguing *to* our basis of truth (e.g., the Bible, evidences for the faith, etc.), rather than *from* our basis of truth. We should be eager to communicate the gospel because it is the power of God for the salvation of all who believe. However, those who so frequently complain about having the Bible shoved down their throats do so for a reason. As we bring Scripture into the conversation, we do so as humble messengers prayerfully discerning what God is doing.

Be a listener. In the postmodern world the successful communicator knows how to listen. Evangelism involves listening to people's stories and ideas, asking good questions and helping our friends discover truth, as opposed to simply informing them of the truth and asking them to believe it. "We affirm that witness does not preclude dialogue, but invites it, and that dialogue does not preclude witness but extends and deepens it."[41] Good listening builds bridges to good spiritual conversation.

Similarly, developing the faith of believers involves listening well as they wrestle with difficult teachings, such as the presence of evil in the world, the nature of eternal punishment and the exclusive allegiance Christ demands. This generation is unsatisfied with being spoon-fed the "right" answers, seeking instead spiritual guides to walk with them as they process these deep questions. We also need to help them discern the ways God has wired them to connect with him. Rather than offer one-size-fits-all approaches to spirituality, we need to discover along with them which practices, relationships and experiences best serve them as they grow into life with Jesus.

Be a storyteller. It is interesting to note that in the New Testament, Jesus spoke primarily in stories, while Paul spoke primarily in rational arguments. First-century Hebrews had a more dynamic mindset that emphasized action, while first-century Greeks had a more static mindset that emphasized contemplation and thought. Consequently, Jesus spoke in story, capturing the imaginations of the Jewish people, and Paul spoke in abstractions, engaging the rational minds of those in the Greek world.[42] While Westerners in the modern era were more like rational Greeks, postmodern people are more like the ancient Hebrews, looking for a faith that is reasonable but that also captures their imagination. Consequently, we must learn to tell God's story in ways that intersect with the stories of our hearers.

Brian McLaren gives four excellent suggestions for effective storytelling.[43] First, listen to their story. Show genuine respect and interest, ask good questions (e.g., Where are you spiritually? Do you have a religious background? What are your thoughts about God?). Be careful to talk with, rather than at, people. Second, share your story. It is good to approach this gently (even asking permission to share), but people with some spiritual interest are generally eager to hear others' personal experiences. Third, tell them God's story. Having listened to your friend's story, there frequently are intersections with stories about Jesus or that Jesus told that can be shared. Fourth, be an inviter, bringer and includer. If the person is interested in learning more, invite him or her to participate in some aspect of church (if the person is ready) or in informal gatherings where believers are present.

Similarly, as people become followers of Jesus their growth is enhanced by an approach to spiritual formation that lives in the real-life stories of those around them, as opposed to getting information about God in a more impersonal, didactic way. As we help others grow as disciples, we need to be generous in sharing our own experiences of being transformed, the means we utilize, our failures, successes, struggles, triumphs, joys, sorrows and fears.

Make room for mystery and ambiguity. Graham Johnston compares the modern era's approach to mystery and the transcendent to the ultralogical Mr. Spock from *Star Trek* (who would accept only what could be explained by reason) and to the supposedly supernatural elements of *Scooby Doo* (which were always shown to be illusions using hidden wires and rubber masks). Contrast this with the *X-Files* or *LOST*, which proclaims to a new generation that life's mysteries are not only real and ever-present, but are complex and beyond our ability to unravel.[44]

Postmoderns recognize that the world consists of more than the physical, and they long for the transcendent. They do not want a "God shrunken to fit modern tastes," but a God who is big and transcendent and capable of embodying the mysteries of the universe we live in.[45] They need to have their imaginations captured along with their intellects. In the postmodern world we must embrace the fact that God is bigger than we can fully comprehend, allow our faith to be filled with awe and wonder, and choose to live in (rather than alleviate) the tension that comes from the many paradoxes inherent to a faith as rich as ours.

Make an ally of pop culture. The postmodern generations are extremely well-versed in and deeply affected by popular culture. In many ways film and music are the lingua franca of our day, and being conversant in these media will provide a means for speaking about spiritual issues.

For many in the church, venturing into popular culture is quite unnerving. While the task of communicating the gospel in terms the culture can understand should not be taken without some measure of prayerful caution, the church must not allow excessive fear of pop culture to prevent it from doing so. Refraining from presenting the gospel in culturally appropriate packaging does not automatically mean that we are presenting a "purer" gospel. On the contrary, we may be presenting the gospel in cultural packaging that was once popular but no longer is. In the same way that Jesus related truths about his Father's kingdom to things his hearers were familiar with (fishing, agriculture, shepherding, etc.), we will do well to communicate with our culture utilizing media that is familiar to them.

Embrace the mystical element of faith. Christianity has a long and rich history of experiential faith. The modern church treats the more experiential aspects of the faith with suspicion, but postmoderns want a faith they can feel. Consequently, we should make use of classic spiritual disciplines like meditation, fasting and solitude, and draw on the faith practices of Christians from different centuries and differing traditions.

Of course there are dangers and excesses to be avoided here as well, but with wisdom and biblical discernment we must not be afraid to enter in. We should expect that participants in a solidly biblical faith will experience God, not just acquire facts about him.

Avoid a shrunken gospel. In sharing the gospel with postmodern people, we must be careful to present a full picture of the message and avoid any kind of bait-and-switch approach. Evangelism does not merely invite people to heaven but to participate in God's world-changing mission. And as they grow, we must continue to lead these believers into a vision of discipleship that involves living as kingdom people, being changed by Jesus into his likeness.

CONCLUSION

For an apologetic to be truly embodied, it needs to permeate the ministries of the church. This implies that we are being spiritually formed as disciples of Jesus, are engaged in God's mission of making disciples of others, and are living out God's mission in a way that fits the cultural context.

For an embodied apologetic to be effective, it cannot be an occasional practice of the church. It needs to be woven into the fabric of the church's life, practice and teaching. Next we will consider how to integrate an embodied apologetic into our church's primary ministry structures, and make embodying the faith part of the ordinary practice of those who belong to our congregations.

Apologetic	Experiential	Communal	Enacted
Need	Transcendence	Community	Purpose
Ministry structure	Worship gatherings	Small groups, etc.	Compassion and justice

Figure 4.1. Elements of an embodied apologetic

ɔ

5

Experiential Faith

*Since we are receiving a kingdom that cannot be shaken, let us be
thankful, and worship God acceptably with reverence and awe.*

HEBREWS 12:28

*The perfect church service would be one we were almost
unaware of; our attention would have been on God.*

C. S. LEWIS, *LETTERS TO MALCOLM*

Some of my favorite moments in ministry include watching people
who are far from God meet him in worship. At times it's almost
like I can see a breakthrough taking place—faith being restored,
open wounds being healed, an "aha" moment as a teaching from
Scripture connects, the body and blood of Christ ingested for the
first time.

One young lady was returning to faith after years of absence.
She had given up on God in the midst of some horrific wounds,
but had tentatively begun attending our worship gatherings with
some friends. As we worshiped one night, I felt as if I was watching her healing take place in real time. Everyone around her was
seated, but she was on her feet, singing, smiling, tears sliding
down her cheeks. She was finding faith again.

Another young woman, filled with shame for the ways she had
abused her body, quietly wept as the refreshment of repentance
filled her soul. Another attended for months, slipping in late and

leaving early so he wouldn't have to talk to anyone, but also because worship was so emotionally overwhelming for him. The dissonance between the life he was leading and the pressing of the Holy Spirit against him in worship was too much. I watched one night as finally he came to the communion table and began to trust God enough to let him in. A young atheist began attending only out of sheer pain following his wife's affair. When he eventually received Christ, it wasn't the logical arguments that convinced him (though they helped)—but the undeniable sense that God was actually present with the church as we worshiped.

This is my story too. During a turning point in college I began to attend church for the first time in years. I too made a point of coming late and leaving early so I wouldn't have to talk to any Christians. There was much I heard there that I had questions about, and even though I had no desire to worship a God I was unsure of, a big reason I continued to return was the worship. Simply put, when I was with these people as they worshiped, I had a hard time convincing myself that they didn't know God. There was something very real happening that I could feel and simply could not deny.

Something very powerful takes place when God's people gather to worship. As the story of our faith is rehearsed, celebrated, taught from Scripture and enacted in the sacraments, we come face to face with the mysterious reality that there is One greater in our midst. Worship gatherings are one of the church's primary ministry structures for disciplemaking. Here followers of Jesus are slowly but definitely shaped in their spiritual formation, and for those outside the faith the worship gathering can serve as a powerful experiential apologetic.

WORSHIP AS EXPERIENTIAL APOLOGETIC

Genuine experiences of worship are powerful tools for reaching lost people, as well as for building up believers. In song, prayer, preaching and teaching, art, personal story and communion, we sometimes find ourselves in what C. S. Lewis referred to as a "thin place," where the veil between the physical and spiritual worlds suddenly seems permeable.[1] In a postmodern world where "experience replaces reason, feeling is more important than form, and the heart triumphs over the head,"[2] experiencing God's presence in the praises of his people carries a weight that an evidential argument typically does not.

Scripture attests that worship is an experience God makes available to those who don't yet know him. There are numerous Old Testament references to this and frequent calls to the nation of Israel to declare God's glory in the presence of the pagan world.

> I will praise you, Lord, among the nations;
>   I will sing of you among the peoples.
> For great is your love, reaching to the heavens;
>   your faithfulness reaches to the skies.
> Be exalted, O God, above the heavens;
>   let your glory be over all the earth.
>   (Ps 57:9-11; cf. Ps 96:10; 18:49)

The nearness of Israel's God and the righteousness of his laws served as demonstrations to Israel and its neighbors that Israel's God is the true God. "What other nation is so great as to have their gods near them the way the LORD our God is near us whenever we pray to him? And what other nation is so great as to have such righteous decrees and laws?" (Deut 4:7-8).

It was expected that there would be strangers and aliens both witnessing and at times participating in the Lord's worship (Num 15:14; Deut 26:10-11). One function of the temple and its worship was to serve as a witness to the nations (1 Kings 8:41-43; 2 Chron 9:3-8).[3] These aspects of worship fit naturally with the Jewish expectation, based on the Abrahamic promise, that all people would be blessed by the God of Israel.

In the New Testament, Paul reiterates this teaching in his letter to the Romans when he quotes from a number of these Old Testament passages:

> Therefore I will praise you among the Gentiles;
>> I will sing praises of your name. . . .
> Rejoice, you Gentiles, with his people. . . .
> Praise the Lord, all you Gentiles,
>> let all the peoples extol him. (Rom 15:9-11)

Paul also admonishes the Corinthian church to worship in such a way that inquirers are not alienated and can understand what is happening. Paul's hope is that the worship experience would cause inquirers to conclude "God is really among you!" and to become worshipers of God (1 Cor 14:25).

Christian worship is a rich and varied practice, with different shapes, forms and emphases moving to the fore in different times and cultures. As we consider the role the worship gathering plays in our twenty-first-century mission field, what theological and practical aspects of our worship will emerge as especially important? And what are the characteristics of worship that will best contribute to its function as an experiential apologetic?

GOD CENTERED

Worship is first and foremost for God. Glorifying and enjoying our Creator and Savior is our highest calling. Even in talking about its value in drawing unbelievers to Christ and in forming believers into the image of Christ, we need to remember that these good things are a byproduct of worship and not its central purpose. Our worship must remain focused on God and not become a means to another end.

When we are attempting to reach those outside the church, it is

easy to lose sight of this and become overly focused on finding
ways to give our worship a broader appeal. But the power to bring
real spiritual change in believers and unbelievers is the result of
genuine worship taking place, not of manufacturing a hip, flashy
or entertaining gathering. C. S. Lewis speaks to this:

> Novelty, simply as such, can have only an entertainment
> value. And [people] don't go to church to be entertained.
> They go to use the service, or if you prefer, to enact it. Every
> service is a structure of acts and words through which we
> receive a sacrament, or repent, or supplicate, or adore. . . . As
> long as you notice, and have to count, the steps, you are not
> yet dancing but only learning to dance. A good shoe is a shoe
> you don't notice. Good reading becomes possible when you
> need not consciously think about eyes, or light, or print, or
> spelling. The perfect church service would be one we were
> almost unaware of; our attention would have been on God.[4]

I'm not saying cultural relevance is unimportant; only that it
must serve the end of truly helping people worship, not simply
making our church more hip than the one down the street. Our
goal must be to help people see God and cry out to him from the
heart, not to engineer an event to elicit a desired reaction or result
from people.

At Life Covenant Church we use the metaphor of the lenses in
a pair of glasses.[5] The lens is not meant to be seen; it is meant to
be seen through. A good lens doesn't call attention to itself—its
purpose is to help us focus on an object. As worship leaders (musi-
cians, preachers, prayer leaders, etc.), our goal is to help people
focus on God. We are at our best when people are no longer aware
of us but see Jesus more clearly through us.

Many of us need to adjust the way we evaluate our worship.
Dan Kimball points us in the right direction when he says our
criteria should not be "I enjoyed that" but "I encountered God

today," or "I became more of a disciple of Jesus today."[6] The goal must be to help people grow as worshipers of God and apprentices of Jesus, not as consumers of religious programs. If our gatherings only serve to validate the culture's hyper-individualism and consumerism, the body gathered will neither be worshiping well nor helping people move closer to Jesus.

AUTHENTIC

In his study of younger evangelicals, Robert Webber finds that their worship is characterized by a strong reaction to an entertainment approach to worship, and a longing for an experience of God's presence.[7] These stand in distinction to and are in part a reaction against trends that are often seen in baby-boomer churches. "The [boomers'] bywords were 'big,' 'flashy,' 'slick,' 'entertaining,' and 'What's in it for me?' The younger evangelical's bywords are 'real,' 'genuine,' 'relational,' 'honest,' 'mix it up,' and 'What can I do for others?' "[8]

In many boomer churches worship is watered down in an attempt to make it more palatable to those who are seeking. Being "seeker friendly" means religious symbols are removed or minimized, church buildings are made less churchy, difficult theological language is avoided in songs and sometimes difficult topics are avoided. The spiritual life was made to appear "normal" and less mysterious. This approach appeals primarily to those with some church background who can return and find, as many church slogans put it, that "church was never like this!"[9] To the postmodern generations, however, such services feel plastic and inauthentic.

With the postmodern generations the approach is in many ways the opposite of this. Worship certainly must be understandable and should be culturally relevant, but must not be diluted or sugarcoated. Those who are coming as inquirers do not want something devoid of spiritual mystery that looks identical to the rest of life. If they are there at all, it's because they are looking for spiritual reality. And ironically, they often reject Christianity because it does not appear spiritual enough! Worship in our churches must be *worship*. It cannot be entertainment, an evangelistic gimmick or an attempt to mimic culture.

This flips "seeker sensitive" on its head. With the postmodern generations we best embody our apologetics when we plan our worship gathering primarily with *believers* in mind. Even as we work to make our gathering accessible to those outside the faith, in our congregation the goal is primarily to lead believers into an experience of seeing God clearly and responding to his greatness. It is the authenticity of the Christian worship experience, more than its accessibility for non-Christians, that lends itself to an experience the non-Christian finds compelling.

CONTEXTUALIZED

While I consider issues of style to be secondary to authenticity, it is deeply important that our worship is culturally relevant as well. Chuck Smith Jr. expresses a missional outlook on this:

> There is no biblical mandate for a church to make use of the musical forms of its host culture . . . [however] a church that wants to provide worship in the *lingua franca* of mainstream culture, that is concerned with how intelligible it is to its host culture, will be interested in the current style, trends, and music of that culture. . . .
>
> Will the church's music reveal the relevance of our faith to people on the outside, or will it make us look like aliens?[10]

To be effective at making disciples of the postmodern generations, we must worship in a way that allows them to cry out to God in their own heart language. This is particularly true when it comes to music. The church is tempted to preserve and institutionalize the forms of worship that have become precious to them.

Erwin McManus observes, "Perhaps the greatest tragedy of our time is that we have kept our pews and lost our children."[11] Without discarding the riches of worship from previous generations, we must allow musical worship to take on the indigenous forms of those we are reaching with the gospel.

When I was in college ministry, I was setting up chairs one night while the band rehearsed for our worship gathering. I recognized the lyrics, but the music was totally different. They were playing it the way they would have if they were jamming in their garage, and having a great time doing it. Finally the leader stopped everyone and said, "Okay, let's get serious," and with pained expressions the others nodded and began to play the song the way they always had in the past. I think I dropped the chair I was holding and practically yelled at them, "Guys! Lead us in this song the way you would if you were just worshiping at home by yourself." They did, and from that point on our worship was never the same. It began to evolve into something far more natural, beautiful and heartfelt. It moved from religious duty to loving communication with God.

The goal here is not to mimic popular culture and therefore better market the church. On the contrary, the idea is to let worship grow in our churches in ways that are indigenous rather than as "badly fitted imports from somewhere else."[12] As we do our best to eliminate stylistic and cultural barriers, we free people to worship in the language of their heart.

Transcendent and Immanent

Another aspect of our worship that is important as we consider how we embody our apologetic is the issue of God's transcendence and immanence. When we look at the hymns that have been the mainstay of worship in the Western world for generations, the greatest weight is put on transcendence—God's greatness, and the awe and reverence it properly evokes. Baby boomers, perhaps in

reaction to this, prefer focusing on God's immanence—his nearness and gentle invitation to intimacy.

As we consider this dynamic with the postmodern generation,
we need to consciously pursue both reverence and intimacy, transcendence and immanence in our worship. Postmoderns certainly
want to experience God as near, but at the same time they react
against God being reduced or tamed to look like the "Buddy Jesus"
of the film *Dogma*.

As Eugene Peterson says, reverence and intimacy need each
other, and in the Scriptures they weave together seamlessly.[13]
When Jesus teaches his disciples to pray, he tells them to call on
God as *Abba* (intimacy), and yet in the same breath reminds them
of the holiness of God's name (reverence). In Matthew's account of
the resurrection (Mt 28:9), the women at the tomb meet the risen
Jesus and instinctively fall and worship (reverence), yet they dare
to touch his feet (intimacy). John's Gospel adds another intimate
detail, when Jesus calls Mary, she calls him "Rabboni," an affec-
tionate, almost playful title (Jn 20:16). And John's Gospel ends
with an intimate portrait of Peter and Jesus ("do you love me?"),
that is tinged with reverence as well ("None of the disciples dared
ask him, 'Who are you?' "). This is the God postmoderns long to
worship—the one who is both transcendent and immanent.

HISTORICALLY ROOTED

Perhaps as a result of the fragmentation and individualism that
marked their formative years, the postmodern generations have a
deep appreciation for the more ancient aspects of the faith. Many
postmoderns feel disconnected from their parent's generation, and
the rootedness that comes from knowing that they are part of a
rich historic community adds depth to their faith.

Consequently there is great interest in the spiritual practices,
symbols and teachings of earlier generations of the church. The
Christian faith gains credibility as we connect our faith to the

early church and as we help our churches see themselves as part of the great cloud of witnesses that has followed Jesus for two thousand years. When we introduce aspects of ancient liturgy, spiritual disciplines and the stories of historic figures in the church, we invite our people to be part of this history.

Many of us are comfortable reaching back as far as the Reformation, but Robert Webber also sees interaction with the early church as especially important for our twenty-first-century context:

> No Christian dare wrestle with postmodern thought until he or she has studied classical Christian thought. To give special attention to the period of classical Christian thought is to be orthodox, evangelical, and ecumenical. Novel ideas of the faith will come and go, but the classical Christian tradition will endure. Thus the primary reason to return to the Christian tradition is because it is truth that has the power to speak to a postmodern world. Early Christian teaching is simple and uncluttered, it cuts through the complexities of culturized Christianity and allows what is primary and essential to surface.[14]

Worship, especially the type that serves as an apologetic, will have one foot in the ancient world and one foot in the future.[15]

SYMBOLIC

Our culture's shift toward postmodernism has changed the way communication occurs. In the premodern (largely preliterate) age, symbol and story were key methods of communicating gospel truths. Consequently, the sacraments took on tremendous importance in enacting the meaning of the faith, as did the biblical stories depicted in the community's art. Parents and priests educated children by telling the Bible's stories as depicted in the symbols, art, stained glass and other objects present in the church. Symbolic communication was particularly important for communicating a sense of awe and wonder in God. Mystery played a large role in understanding the faith.[16]

In the modern age, easier access to printed media made the Bible accessible. The written word became the dominant means of communication and symbolic communication diminished. Mystery tended to give way to explanation and played a smaller role in understanding the faith. Reasoned, systematic understandings of Christian truth dominated story, and a sense of mystery took a back seat to the clarifying power of the spoken and written word. Churches reflected this shift as the pulpit replaced the Lord's Table as the focal point of worship.

In the postmodern era there is a deep longing for a recovery of awe and wonder. Consequently, "It may be said broadly that the story of Christianity moves from a focus on mystery in the classical period, to institution in the medieval era, to individualism in the Reformation era, to reason in the modern era, and now, in the postmodern era, back to mystery."[17]

With the advent of hypertext and visual media, communication is changing once again. Though still dominant, word-centered communication has lost some if its power. Words have not been replaced, but there is a significant rise in the importance of images, experience and narrative, and a return to symbolic communication.[18] Due in large part to the use of symbol in visual storytelling (especially film, television and the Internet), we are once again using symbols for communicating profound truths. And as we increasingly recognize that the supernatural is not easily systematized, mystery has returned as an important part of faith.[19]

The ways we take in and process information have changed to include these other forms, and consequently the church must make this type of communication part of its approach as well. Chuck Smith Jr. says, "What materials do we need to construct a postmodern faith? Besides the *message* of premodern faith, and the *reasons* of modern faith, we need to supply the right *signs or symbols* for a postmodern faith."[20]

SHAPING OUR WORSHIP GATHERINGS

Life defines *worship* as *our response to God revealing himself to us.* This simple statement has gone a long way in shaping the way we approach Sundays.

First, it led us to invert what most of us knew as a "normal" order of worship. Many of us are from traditions where the sermon was the main event, and musical and other worship forms were treated almost as a warm-up for the message. As our understanding of worship took hold, however, it made more sense to begin our service by reading and teaching the Scriptures (God revealing himself to us), and then to build the rest of our time around responding to that word. So our typical liturgy consists of prayer, a brief time of musical worship, a sermon, and then a more substantial time of musical worship and other responses. As we worship in song, people are invited to use the space to move around, find a more private spot to pray or sing, to take communion (there are several stations around the room to do this), to give financially, to be prayed for (there is a station for this as well), or occasionally to respond in some other way more specific to that night's message.

Second, our understanding of worship has caused us to value a sense of sacredness. As we gather, we recognize that Jesus is truly present, knowing that we can meet God, hear from him and respond with full hearts. The room itself is dimly lit, and there is space around the sides where people can move about freely as we respond. We have a ministry team who oversees the aesthetics of our worship gatherings, and they arrange the stations, create and arrange artistic displays, project visual art to accompany song lyrics and suggest other avenues for people's response.

Finally, our focus on worship—God revealing himself and our

response—has led our congregation to value simplicity in worship. While we value excellence, we are minimalists in many ways and tend to avoid splashy visual or musical displays or anything that might seem pretentious. Our goal is simply to communicate God's revelation as clearly as we can, and then provide space for people to respond.

Here are some of the elements we incorporate into our worship. Some of these occur nearly every week (musical worship, teaching, communion), while others are more occasional, but they represent the spectrum of what occurs at Life's worship gatherings.

Prayer. Conversation with God stands at the center of the spiritual life. When we come together as a worshiping community, we want our time to be permeated with this conversation. We are led in prayer by worship leaders and teachers, individuals present their needs to God in response to the work he is doing in their heart, and during the responsive portion of our gathering there is a station where people can receive prayer for their needs.

Praying for one another reminds us of our need to receive from God, to experience his grace in the variety of life situations we find ourselves in, and our interdependence with others in the body. While Scripture certainly affirms that God hears individual's prayers, we are meant to function as part of a body, and we need others to intercede for and with us as well. Too often we misunderstand the Reformers' "priesthood of all believers" to mean that we don't need a priest. On the contrary, God makes us all priests, not that we each might be a priest to ourselves but that we may be priests for one another. It is a "confession of mutuality," an acknowledgement that God has made us to fill that role in each other's life. Regular prayer for one another helps to teach us this.[21]

Music. Love is hard to express. Whether we are talking about the passion we feel for our spouse, the heart tug we have for our children or the grateful joy we feel toward God, words often fail us when we try to explain what is in our hearts. A well-written song can give us a verbal framework to hang our heart's longings on, and a beautiful piece of music can help us connect otherwise passionless words to the emotions God's greatness elicits. Music and song open the door for us to express our hearts to our Creator in fuller and richer ways.

Similarly, music touches our emotions, allowing us to open up and be more vulnerable before God. At times our hearts remain shut in the face of spoken words, but music has a way of bypassing our defenses and reaching those tender spots we would rather not expose. Sometimes God's gentle whisper breaks through in the melody of a song.

Teaching and preaching. Jesus told his followers that part of disciplemaking is "teaching them to obey everything I have commanded" (Mt 28:20). We take seriously the role of Scripture as God's revelation and our source of authority, and seek to live lives of obedience.

Our hope is that as we come together, we will let the Scriptures read us, and that God will speak through them in leading us into more Christlike lives. I like how Doug Pagitt expresses this: "We focus our efforts on trying to figure out if our lives could be relevant to the story of God, not if the Bible can be relevant to our lives."[22]

Twenty-first-century preachers must become skilled at exegeting three sources: the biblical text, the surrounding culture and the human heart. Effective communication connects biblical truths with the deep cries of our hearts in ways that are culturally relevant. Among other things, this means that we major on storytelling (which serves to draw listeners into an experience as well as impart truth), and we make worship a place where members of the body share their stories. Stories of God at work are a powerful apologetic and serve to build community. We try to approach preaching less as giving answers and more as raising the right questions, and to preach in such a way that the mysteries of God are not alleviated, but embraced.[23]

This does not involve sugarcoating difficult truths. Postmodern listeners hunger for a thorough teaching of the Bible and a full experience of the faith. Our preaching needs to be theologically rich, socially minded and aimed at both the heart and outward actions. Dan Kimball is right when he says, "Emerging generations are starving for deeper teaching, and our job is to respect them enough to give it to them."[24]

Communion. Jesus gave his church a meal of celebration and remembrance. One of the most significant acts of worship for believers is sharing in this communion together. In taking the bread and the cup, we participate in and proclaim the death and resurrection of Jesus, remembering the price he paid that we could know him.

Participation in the Lord's Supper is a powerful form of worship, with the capacity to contribute greatly to our spiritual formation. Unfortunately, in many of our churches, it has been reduced to a mere intellectual recall of Christ's suffering. In our effort to avoid the errors of Catholic theology, we have too often removed any sense of experiencing the real presence of Christ at the Lord's Table (the same could be said of baptism as well). The mystery has been removed, and we are left with little expectation of actually meeting God. In reality, communion is a powerful time to both remember and experience the actual presence of Jesus as promised to his followers (Mt 28:20).

How much better would it be to emphasize this sacrament and allow it to stand as a "visual sermon," symbolically proclaiming the Word of God?[25] I am impressed with the example of Robert Webber, who, when Wheaton students came to him for counseling, would admit that he had nothing to offer them in their pain, but counseled them instead to run to the Table of the Lord. "It is there," he told them, "that God can and does touch his people in a healing way."[26]

Communion is celebrated weekly at Life. Most weeks it is served at stations around the room where congregants (sometimes alone, but often with family or friends) take the elements as they respond in worship. Other times the elements are passed, or people form a line as the elements are served from the front. In any case, we participate in this worship as a community formed and united by Christ's sacrifice. And as we regularly retell and participate in Christ's story through communion, God further shapes our new life as members of his family.

Giving. Many people are surprised when they realize how much Jesus talked about money. Our relationship to our possessions plays a very prominent role in our relationship to God, and we see in Scripture that followers of Jesus are marked by generosity, simplicity and trust in a God who provides. At Life we see giving as a part of our worship, a tangible response of thanks to God and a key means by which God shapes us.

Our church has proven to be a very generous congregation, giving sacrificially from the beginning. In our first three-and-a-half years, in addition to funding our own ministry, congregants have financially and prayerfully supported two new church plants in neighboring cities, and have begun microenterprise work in Africa.

Story. The church has many voices. Our individual stories of how God has worked and is working in and through us are powerful and need to be shared. We regularly make space in our gatherings to hear from one another how God is working, and several times a year there are open sharing nights where people's own stories of God's work take the place of a sermon.

There is a certain messiness to this practice, which we deeply value. We invite people to share whether or not their delivery is polished, and we encourage people to share stories that are still in process and do not yet have a happy ending. We find this vulnerability (which those of us who share the teaching and preaching role try to model as well) is one way we are able to foster a sense of authenticity in our worship.

Psalms. C. S. Lewis said, "The most valuable thing the Psalms do for me is to express that same delight in God which made David dance."[27] Reading and praying the Psalms is often incorporated into our worship gatherings. These songs and prayers have guided Christ's church from its inception. They teach us how to pray, show us how to bring our whole hearts into the act of worship, give us a vocabulary for joyful praise, remind us that grieving in God's presence is every bit as spiritual as rejoicing and confirm that God would rather hear our dark thoughts than have us hide them. The Psalms keep our spirituality grounded in the real events of life.

We have found that praying a psalm together can be meaningful as an act of worship, in addition to serving to introduce our congregation to this as a devotional discipline. Eugene Peterson considers prayerful meditation on the Psalms to be an essential discipline; it formed the prayer life of both Old and New Testament saints, as well as much of the church in the last two millennia.[28] Dietrich Bonhoeffer saw the Psalms as the "great school of prayer," and believed that as the Psalms are prayed together in corporate worship, the prayer lives of all involved are enriched.[29]

Making the Psalms a part of our worship also allows worship to express the full range of human emotion. It is instructive to note that most modern worship music leans in the direction of joyful celebration, whereas, only about half the Psalms do; the other half express lament. Praying the Psalms together helps us worship God from hearts that are full of either joy or sorrow, and reminds us of our need to be emotionally genuine before God when we pray.

Ancient prayers and writings. We want to remind ourselves that we are part of something very ancient even as we follow God into the future. We believe our faith will be at its best when it is grounded in the church's history and we are learning from believers in other times and places. Consequently, we regularly incorporate ancient prayers, writings, creeds and classic hymns into our gatherings.

Coming from a nonliturgical tradition, I have rarely been comfortable praying other people's prayers. However, in the last few years I have come to appreciate this practice, especially as it pertains to using prayers written by saints of centuries past. It can be difficult to find words to express the heart, and at times those of us who are used to free prayers find ourselves falling into patterns of repetition that can become meaningless and trite. Corporately praying ancient prayers is one way to address this, while also connecting the church to its historical roots.

The worship gathering also presents the opportunity to introduce people to the writings of the spiritual masters of the past. We can expose our churches to their wisdom and nurture a hunger to read and benefit from classic spiritual writers.

Food. There is something special about eating with others. The church is God's family, and we value time spent at the table with one another. As well as opening our homes to one another, we regularly employ "family meals" after worship as an expression of praise and thanks to God.

In doing this we are following the example of Jesus, whose table fellowship served to communicate friendship and acceptance to even the least desirable in society (Lk 7:34). We are also following the lead of the early church, who clearly found common meals to be an important part of their worship and life together (Acts 2:46; 1 Cor 11:17-34), and of the people of Israel, whose regular feasting was done "in the presence of the LORD" as an act of worship (Deut 14:22-26). Similarly, we don't see eating together as something that happens after worship but as part of worship.

Silence. Solitude and silence are foundational disciplines that we must introduce our people to. These disciplines open the door for many of the other spiritual disciplines, and they allow us to get rid of life's "scaffolding" (relationships, material goods, entertainments and diversions) that keep us from looking deeply at ourselves.[30] Few people deliberately make time for silence, and without deliberate planning, silence will not happen in our noisy world.

The discipline of silence is one that can be incorporated into worship. When we interject meaningful periods of silence into a worship gathering, it creates space for reflection and for listening to God. And allowing the congregation moments of silent contemplation during worship reminds us that God is speaking throughout the week if we will only stop and listen.

Art. As people made in the image of a creative God, we have been given a tremendous capacity to create. Many of us communicate best through art, and we want to make space for this kind of expression. In creating an atmosphere for worship, providing visual expressions and symbols of the faith, and providing opportunities for members to share what they have created (poetry, painting, photography, music, sculpture), we believe the creation and enjoyment of art enhances our worship. Art created by those who are part of our church is displayed at our communion stations and as background on slides, and we will sometimes invite an artist to tell the story behind his or her piece.

A refreshing rediscovery of the arts is taking place in many young churches. What was commonly an aid to worship in the ancient church is making a comeback as we transition from a modern to a postmodern era. Craftsmanship and creations of art are a form of worship in Scripture (Ex 31:1-6). Art helps God's people enter into worship (Ex 30). The furnishings of the tabernacle, the beauty of the temple itself and frequent visual events from the burning bush to the spectacle of Pentecost remind us that, throughout Scripture, we see visual experiences accompany and elaborate on God's Word to his people.[31] Centuries later, St.

Bonaventure recognized this and reflected on beauty (both natural and human) as essential to recognizing God's "footprints" in the world, and thus deepening our journey into him.[32] As Martin Luther reportedly said, "Everything preaches."

The worship gathering is an important venue for cultivating both the creation and the enjoyment of art as spiritual disciplines. For those who are gifted in painting, writing poetry, sculpting, composing music, graphic design, filmmaking, photography and other art forms, the creative process is an important part of their own spiritual formation. And enjoying the beauty of what they create serves both artist and non-artist alike in enhancing the revelation that comes from our Creator. Good art helps us see.

Meditation. In our worship gatherings we give people different ways to pray and interact with Scripture. Certain forms of meditation on Scripture that are very useful devotionally can also be incorporated into the worship gathering. Particularly when a shorter passage is used, the ancient practice of lectio divina can be helpful.[33] The Ignatian method of meditation can also be practiced in this setting.[34] The imaginative aspect of this discipline makes it appealing for congregations, and learning to read the Scriptures with a "baptized imagination" can add great value to the devotional life of the believer.[35] Praying "palms up, palms down" as the Quakers do is also a good exercise we practice occasionally, as is Luther's method of Scripture meditation, focused silent attention on God's presence, praying the Psalms, and visual displays of Scripture projected on the screen or displayed at a station.[36]

Benediction. I'm told that Martin Luther said, "You do not dismiss a church—you disperse it." Our gathering formally ends with a benediction, in which we receive by faith God's blessing as we go out into the world to *be* the church, to bless and serve others in the name of Christ, and to live in obedience to the teachings of Jesus. I'm inspired by the words of Ernest Southcott, "The holiest moment of the church service is the moment when God's people—

strengthened by preaching and sacrament—go out of the church door into the world to be the church. We don't go to church; we are the church."[37]

CONCLUSION

Embodied apologetics are experiential. As we consider how we can embed this aspect of our witness in the life of the church, the worship gathering is a key ministry structure. In worship, we bring God the praise he deserves, and as we do so, believers are shaped into the image of Christ and inquirers experience the present reality of God in a unique way.

6

Communal Faith

Your love for one another will prove to
the world that you are my disciples.

JOHN 13:35 NLT

Evangelism is less an invitation to an event and
more of an invitation to enter into community.

DAN KIMBALL, *THE EMERGING CHURCH*

I was midway through college when I began to walk with Jesus. My running from God and absence from the church had lasted about five years, which was plenty of time to really foul up my life. When I returned I was broken in ways that felt beyond repair. I was reeling from the breakup of a three-year relationship marked by bitterness and betrayal, had friends I valued yet the friendships felt hollow, and most of my leisure activities included being intoxicated in one way or another. I was confused by a life that didn't make sense and desperately wanted to find and live what was real.

Of the things God used in putting me back together, none had as much impact as the amazing community of believers that embraced me. There was a small group who welcomed me to join them as they met weekly to study the Bible together, worship, pray and serve others. They were far from perfect. They suffered with their own problems, struggled with all manner of sin and didn't have many of the answers I needed. But they knew God. It was undeniable.

I think I found comfort in seeing that these were not super-Christians who had their acts completely together. They were pretty normal people, but they clearly dealt with life's ups and downs in a much different way than I did. In the midst of very real problems, most seemed to have an underlying joy, a peace that sustained them and a love for others that I wanted to have. And as I began to walk with them, God brought me healing. It was nothing dramatic—a casual word offered over pizza, a friend saying, "I'll pray for you," a suggestion to read this passage or listen to that song—but in the course of simply doing life together God showed up. They were brothers and sisters, and soon I found I was part of the family.

In the years since then I have seen what I experienced repeated hundreds of times. When I ask new believers and those returning to faith what made the biggest difference for them, the answer I hear most often is that it was the people. Similarly, I find that the most significant source of spiritual growth for most believers is the people they are journeying with, be they members of a small group, a mentor or apprentice, accountability partners or simply good spiritual friends.

Expressions of community such as these are one of our congregation's three primary ministry structures. They serve as a crucial vehicle for spiritual formation, and simultaneously function as a communal apologetic for those outside the faith. In this chapter we will explore how this takes place, beginning with a look at the biblical and theological basis for embracing community as a way of life for Jesus' followers.

COMMUNITY AS THEOLOGICAL REALITY

One of our congregation's most cherished values is captured in the word *connectional*. We see authentic, loving community as the indispensable context for our mission. We speak of doing life deeply together, and we pray and labor toward truly living this out.

Terms like *authentic community* are fast becoming buzzwords in danger of losing their meaning. But we see *authentic community* neither as faddish nor as merely desirable. Rather, it's an accurate description of a greater reality—what it truly means to be the church. Living into this reality is the challenge we face.

The church as community is a theological reality. Though we sometimes speak in terms of "creating" community, the fact is that it already has been created through the work of Christ. Our task is not to create it out of thin air but to recognize its presence, and to cultivate an environment that will help that community flourish.

Community is based in the very existence of God. At the heart of the universe—the triune God—we find community. God never existed in relational isolation but from eternity past has existed in joyful community as Father, Son and Holy Spirit. The Eastern Church uses the delightful term *perichoresis* (literally "circle dance") to describe this joyful state of relationship. Out of this cosmic dance, God has created us for relationship with himself, to know him and join in with the rhythms of the universe. Like children born into a healthy marriage, we are created out of the pleasure and deep connectedness that exists in the persons of the Trinity. We were, as Meister Eckhart put it, "created out of the laughter of the Trinity." The church stands as the earthly embodiment of this reality, beckoning the world to join the dance.[1]

This reality is seen in the nature of God and also in the work of Christ. The communal nature of Christ's work is especially reflected in the sacraments. Dallas Willard points out that when Jesus commanded his followers to baptize disciples in the name of the Father, Son and Holy Spirit (Mt 28:19), he was asking us to do more than get them wet. The rite signifies a greater reality, namely, our immersion into the very presence of the Trinity ("baptize them in the *name* . . .") Baptism bears witness to the new life we have entered; a life that is now hidden with Christ in God (Col 3:3).

Scripture proclaims that all have been baptized by one Spirit into one body: Christ's (1 Cor 12:13). In entering this new reality of immersion in the presence of God, we find ourselves connected not only to God but to all others who have undergone this same baptism. The church is the company of the baptized, made up of those who have undergone this same trinitarian immersion. Consequently, our individual names have been caught up into the name of the three-personal God. As Eugene Peterson states it, "At that moment [of baptism] we are no longer merely ourselves by ourselves; from then on we are ourselves in the community of similarly baptized persons."[2]

As Paul called the Ephesian church to live in unity, he reminded them that in Christ they were now parts of the same body, and that even the most formidable boundaries that had separated them had been torn down at the cross (Eph 2:14-16; cf. Col 3:11). Moreover, they shared "one Lord, one faith, one baptism" (Eph 4:3-5). The same waters that washed away their sins washed away their neighbors' sins as well.

In communicating just how intertwined the life of Jesus is with his followers, Paul's language takes on a cosmic flavor. Followers of Jesus are now "in Christ" (a phrase used dozens of times), even as Christ is in us (Col 1:27). We are (even presently!) seated with Jesus in the heavenly realms (Eph 2:6), and our lives are "now hidden with Christ in God" (Col 3:3).

In Jesus we are now joined even more closely than family members who share the same blood ties. As Bonhoeffer put it, "We belong to one another only in and through Jesus Christ."[3] And Thomas Kelly says, "[we] are related to one another through Him, as all mountains go down into the same earth."[4]

The reality of our connectedness in Christ is also reinforced every time we come to the communion table. In holy communion, we declare that "life is found in communion with God and one another."[5] Paul says, "Is not the cup of thanksgiving for which we give thanks a participation in the blood of Christ? And is not the bread that we break a participation in the body of Christ? Because there is one loaf, we, who are many, are one body, for we all partake of the one loaf" (1 Cor 10:16-17).

For the ancient church the tremendous bond that exists between believers was pictured in the communion event. The church has traditionally broken one loaf, reminding us that we are one body. One of the earliest Christian documents, the *Didache*, pictures the loaf as the gathered community of believers,[6] and the early church leader Ignatius saw the Supper as the "great bond between believers."[7] It was significant that they were eating *together*, not merely eating. As the community gathered, their worship began by greeting one another with a holy kiss (itself a meaningful gesture of oneness and a reminder that in being reconciled to God they had been reconciled to one another as well), and culminated with the sharing in the body and blood of the Lord. The church worshiped in the knowledge that they were deeply united and that strained relationships needed to be addressed and cared for. Paul's admonition against participating in communion in an unworthy manner must be read primarily as a warning to those who would sin against the unity of the body (1 Cor 11:17-28).[8]

The waters of baptism and the elements of the Lord's Supper remind us of a fundamental reality: we are in the truest sense an authentic community. Whether or not we feel we are experiencing it at any given time, there is a sense in which fellow believers are more closely connected than blood relatives or friends who know each others' deepest secrets.

This is not to say that a vibrant, life-giving community happens automatically. As with all living things, it must be cultivated and nurtured. This is significantly different, though, from creating a community out of thin air. Christ's church *is* a community, mod-

eled after and born out of the laughter of the Trinity, visualized
and remembered whenever we receive the sacraments.

Community is messy. At its best it involves real people bringing
their truest selves into the presence of others. The sacraments remind us of this messiness—that any community is a "community
in progress." A church is made up of baptized sinners at differing
stages of spiritual progression and will necessarily be an imperfect place. Speaking of her own baptism, Anne Lamott humor-
ously reminds us that we spend much of life trying to look good,
act like put-together people, stay dry and keep from slipping under. Baptism is the opposite of all these things. Baptism is "about
surrender, giving into all those things we can't control; it's a will-
ingness to let go of balance and decorum and get *drenched*."[9] In the
same way, participation in the Lord's Supper reminds us weekly of
our need to seek forgiveness, certainly from God, and often from
our brothers and sisters as well.

Community is messy because grace is messy. The more grace-
full we become as a church, the more freedom people will feel to
be real and the messier life will become. We welcome this. And
ironically, this messiness is part of what attracts emerging generations to the faith.

As we look at this reality we see that a communal apologetic
functions in two interrelated ways. First, as members of the community engage in life-on-life activity with other believers, they are
further shaped into the image of Christ. This is crucial because an
embodied apologetic is only effective as the church looks like Jesus. Second, our expressions of community provide entrances into
the church for those who are longing to connect with God and
others.

Missiologist and church planter Ed Stetzer sums up both the
reality and its implications for mission among postmodern people:
"Community is the love of God manifesting itself in and through
the people of God. That is the advantage the church has in this

postmodern society. You can't fake community; it is the reality of the relationships that makes Christ believable to an unbelieving society."[10]

AUTHENTIC COMMUNITY AS APOLOGETIC

During seminary I served a college ministry near San Diego State University where my responsibilities included overseeing our small groups. Our groups were primarily aimed at strengthening believers, but, as we saw a fair number of nonbelievers find Christ in these groups, we came to see that this was a good environment for evangelism as well. One year I decided we needed small groups that were focused solely on evangelism. We would tailor the biblical content of the groups for those who were seeking, eliminate potential awkward spots (like worship and people praying out loud for one another), and attempt to fill the groups with mostly seekers and a minimal number of believers. We decided to start one of these groups in each of the school's dormitories, and went to work recruiting and training sharp college students to lead them.

At the end of that year we made an observation that reshaped our approach. The seeker small groups had hobbled along, taking intense effort but bearing little fruit. Our ministry's "normal" small groups, however, had continued to thrive and had in fact seen far more seekers trust Christ than those groups we had designed specifically for that purpose!

As we interviewed leaders, group members and new believers, it seemed that the thing missing from the evangelistic small groups that the other small groups had was a deep sense of community. The new believers reported being attracted to the quality of relationships that existed between group members and were impressed with the selflessness and caring that they saw displayed in the groups. They felt like God was present there, and they witnessed real Christians sharing both triumphs and failures as they struggled to live out their faith. They enjoyed the dialogue over the Scriptures (which were not sanitized or hand-picked for them), praying for one another and even worship. As they became part of these communities they became convinced that Jesus was real and put their faith in him.

We had been utilizing a communal apologetic without realizing it. In attempting to make our groups more palatable for those investigating the faith, we accidentally removed one of the elements that most drew seekers: Christians living in authentic community. Robert Webber's summation captures our experience: "The missional church . . . evangelizes primarily through immersing the unchurched in the experience of community. In this community they see, hear, and feel the reality of the faith or 'catch' the faith."[11]

All people were created with a deep need for community. For postmoderns, however, this need is often right on the surface. Among those who research generational characteristics and patterns, this need for community is uniformly cited as a defining characteristic of the younger, more postmodern generations. Among other causes, the breakdown of the family, the tripling of the divorce rate and the rise in dual-income families have elevated community as a conscious need.[12] Sociologist (and Gen Xer) Tom Beaudoin boils it down to this: "[Gen X's] most fundamental question is, 'Will you be there for me?' "[13]

This dynamic creates an evangelistic opportunity for the church. As the people of Christ, created for and living in community, the church is well-positioned to meet this need. Consequently, we find that some of our greatest vehicles for evangelism (as well as for the spiritual formation of believers) are our different expressions of community. Small groups of differing kinds are especially important, as they combine an open environment for investigating the claims of Christ with a community of people with whom a person can belong.

The community that has been transformed by Christ may be our greatest apologetic. The authenticity this generation hungers for is most convincing when seen in a group, not just in an individual. "In the modern era, people came to church and asked, 'Who is God?' but today, if people come to church at all, they ask, 'Who are God's people? How does Christianity cash out in community and practice?' "[14] Inviting outsiders into our small groups allows them the opportunity to belong before they believe, investigating and "trying on" the faith as they come to find that it is real.

> In a small-group setting, unlike a one-time encounter, there is no time constraint to pressure people. . . . Individuals who have little prior knowledge of the gospel or exposure to Christian community especially need time to grow in understanding before they are ready to commit themselves.[15]

If this is the case, it serves to further highlight the need to emphasize spiritual formation as part of discipleship. In living as a new creation we become the apologetic God means us to be. Though we, of course, want what happens in a small group to be understandable to the seeker, ours is not a seeker approach. Much like our worship gatherings, our approach here is to create a space for meaningful community to happen among believers. As authentic Christian community happens and contributes to the Christlikeness of its members, a communal apologetic is created.

BELONGING HAPPENS IN MULTIPLE SPACES

It's interesting to listen to what people mean when they talk about community. A while back I had conversations with three different church members about their community needs and was struck by how different their responses were. One expressed the need to have one or two intimate friends with whom they can share their deepest heart. Another said she has great friends in the church but feels alone on Sundays because those few friends are the only people she knows. The third said what he really needs is more social interaction—the kind of friends you call to go out with on a weekend. Though very different, all three get lumped into the need for community. And most of us are pretty certain that our need is the same others have as well—if I fix what is needed for me, real community will be achieved for everyone else too.

I find that one of my challenges is helping people see that not everyone has the same belonging needs. There is a temptation for churches to find one vehicle (usually a small group ministry) and treat it as a sort of panacea for all of their people's belonging needs. As important as small groups are, they are helpful in meeting certain relational needs, but not all.

I was greatly helped in this by *The Search to Belong*, an innovative book by Joseph Myers.[16] Myers asserts that what we need are relationships that are *significant*, not necessarily relationships that are close or intimate.[17] Though one often equates these concepts, they are not always the same. What makes a relationship significant has less to do with how intimate it is and more to do with that relationship's ability to meet the particular relational needs that currently exist for that person.

Myers details four levels of belonging (public, social, personal, intimate) that contribute to a person's overall sense of belonging. To sense that he or she truly belongs to a given community, the person needs to connect with others in all four of these spaces, find these connections significant and both *commit to* and *participate in* the community.[18]

Each of these areas requires a different number of relationships (public the most, intimate the least), and healthy community is achieved when we find balance in all four of these spaces. Myers pictures this balance with a chemical equation of sorts: $Pu_8S_4P_2I$. Generally speaking, for each intimate relationship we need two personal, four social and eight public relationships.[19]

The public level of belonging refers to a person's involvement in a larger group, like a devoted sports fan in a stadium enjoying the company of other screaming fans, or a marathoner running shoulder to shoulder with thousands of other runners. Though the person might not know anyone else in the stands or at the race, there is a level of camaraderie and belonging that he or she feels. This is an important, though often underestimated, level of community.

Social relationships refer to interactions such as small talk with a neighbor or a person whom we see often enough to know by name, but might stop short of what we would consider a close friendship. This social space is important for deciding who we might want to build a deeper friendship with.

Personal relationships involve sharing private (though not "naked") experiences, thoughts and feelings. These are good friends, which is often what we have in mind when we speak of our need for community.

In intimate relationships we share our "naked" thoughts, feelings and experiences with another person. Though churches often promote intimate relationships, we can realistically sustain only a few of these. If all of our relationships were intimate, it would create a very unhealthy situation.[20]

If Myers is correct in this, then our strategy will entail creating an atmosphere where people can grow significant relationships in *all four* of these spaces. Rather than promoting a model where true community happens when people are "close," we will encourage relationships in all four spheres. We will listen well to those in our churches to discern what kind of belonging they most need and direct them accordingly, avoiding the tendency to force them into a small group (or other form) if it is not appropriate.[21]

Different ministry structures can be utilized to cultivate an atmosphere conducive to belonging. If done well, the worship gathering can promote belonging on public and social levels. Small groups and accountability groups can be very effective at promot-

ing personal and even intimate belonging, and many also fill social belonging needs. Ministries of compassion and justice, in
bringing people together for a common purpose, are effective at
promoting social belonging, as are social events and hospitality
dinners. These and other connecting events provide the foundation for people to discern if they want to move into deeper
relationships.

CULTIVATING AN ENVIRONMENT FOR COMMUNITY

In his classic work *Life Together*, Dietrich Bonhoeffer writes that
one of the greatest enemies to community is our *dream* of community. As believers we often come into a new church or group
with noble ideals and images of what that community should be
like, and of the kind of blessing it will be to us and others. Consequently, when we find that our dream community is full of real
people with messy lives, the temptation is to love the dream more
than the real thing. "God's grace speedily shatters such dreams,"
Bonhoeffer writes. "The sooner this shock of disillusionment
comes to an individual and a community the better for both."[22]
When we love ideal (and therefore, imaginary) people rather than
the real people, it leads to a grumbling, dissatisfied spirit that
eventually does harm to us and to those around us. "He who loves
his dream of a community more than the Christian community
itself becomes a destroyer of the latter, even though his personal
intentions may be ever so honest and earnest and sacrificial."[23]

The kind of life-giving community we long for comes not by
wishing we had different (easier?) people to love, or by searching
for yet another group that meets our needs (as we perceive those
needs), but as we love the real, messed-up people around us and
invite them to love us back.

Making expressions of community a primary structure of the
church puts people into close proximity with one another and
helps to frustrate false dreams and correct our presuppositions.

They help us enter common life "not as demanders but as thankful recipients."[24] At Life Covenant Church we utilize several ministry structures that help us cultivate community, and in so doing better embody our apologetic.

Commitment/membership. The emerging generations are notorious nonjoiners. We don't want to make plans for Friday on a Wednesday because a better offer might come on Thursday. In the local church, young believers are increasingly aware of the effects of this American consumerist mentality on church life, yet still struggle with being fickle, slow to commit and quick to shift allegiance. One professor of religion has described this generation as spiritual tourists, staying on the move and picking up souvenirs as we go, rather than claiming any one place (or congregation) as home.[25]

In the New Testament the church is always envisioned as an identifiable group of people, not merely an abstract reality or invisible body. The view that one can claim membership in the universal, invisible body of Christ without identifying with a visible community of Christ followers would not be recognized by the New Testament writers. As Eugene Peterson says, "We can no more be a Christian and have nothing to do with the church than we can be a person and not be in a family. . . . It is part of the fabric of redemption."[26]

In our congregation we have come to see membership as a truly valuable tool for spiritual formation. We have begun calling out our generation's fickleness and calling believers to make a significant commitment. This is radically countercultural, serves to remedy the consumer mentality that plagues the church and aids our growth into Christlikeness. And our young adults are eating up the challenge.

This marks a real shift in my thinking. I used to think membership was a tremendous waste of time ("God knows I'm committed—why do I have to attend a boring class and have my commitment rubber-stamped by the church?") and wasn't planning on having membership at Life. But when I read some of the ancient monastics, I saw the benefit that could come from an approach to membership that infused it with deeper meaning and that made radical demands of its members.

Monks are better known for their practice of solitude than their practice of community. In reality, though, the monks were keenly aware of their need for others in spiritual formation. The Rule of Saint Augustine (the earliest of monastic rules) has some instruction on individual practices but is devoted primarily to instruction on how to live together. The community was seen as more important than the individual, and primacy was given to practices (such as simplicity and other-centeredness) that would nurture and protect spiritual friendships.[27]

Even the desert fathers, who were renowned for their radical pursuit of solitude, made a point to spend time with other solitaries so that they could strengthen one another through table fellowship, saying common prayers and celebrating Mass together. True hermits were the exception.[28]

The practice of community as a spiritual discipline was greatly enhanced in the sixth century by Saint Benedict (perhaps the most influential figure in the history of monasticism). For the first few centuries of monastic life, monks lived by the common vows of poverty, chastity and obedience. To these three Benedict added stability: "the vow to remain where God had placed you, to persist in community, even when the community did not please you personally, to develop the disciplines to remain where God wanted you to be."[29] Benedict sought to counter the practice of many monks who moved from one monastery to the next without committing to any level of belonging. Monks were known to move on if they had a conflict with another brother or preferred another abbey for its abbot, beds or even its wine![30]

The situation that Benedict sought to remedy has a familiar

ring as we think of the flabby commitment exhibited in many local churches today. Too often Christians see themselves more as consumers of than contributors to the church. For the vast majority of churches (and to the disappointment of most pastors), growth and shrinking attendance consists mainly of transfers to and from other local congregations.

More and more I am convinced that our growth as Jesus' disciples is dependent on a commitment to belong to a community of believers. If Jesus defined the greatest commandment as loving God and people, it seems that much of the growth that God would work in us cannot happen apart from the joys and trials of living deeply with other people we are learning to love. To paraphrase the apostle John, we cannot love God apart from loving our brothers and sisters (1 Jn 4:20-21). And Paul speaks of believers reaching maturity and fullness in Christ only as they are all engaged in using the gifts God has given them (Eph 4:11-14; cf. Philemon 6; Heb 10:25). Spiritual formation is a group project.

It is regrettable that some within the emerging church have adopted an ecclesiology that sees commitment to a local congregation as unimportant as long as the individual is committed to Christ and connects in some way with other believers. Belonging to an identifiable congregation gives way (as George Barna recently put it) to the "personal church of the individual" as each believer weaves together different options for his or her own life of faith.[31] Contrary to this view, committed involvement in a congregation is vital to our formation. Loving real people is hard, and life in a congregation is messy, but this does not mean the local church should be abandoned. As Todd Hunter says, they must not be eliminated but redeemed.[32]

In seeking membership at Life, a person is saying that they believe God is calling them to be an apprentice of Jesus in this particular time and place, in the midst and with the help of this particular community of people. We acknowledge that while we belong to the universal church, we are not meant to grow alone. God calls us to live our faith in a particular local expression of the church, and we need to commit to that local body. Such a commitment grounds our walk with Christ in reality, and keeps it from being reduced to a skin-deep faith separate from the experience of brothers and sisters living together.

Membership at our church entails a commitment to both orthodoxy and orthopraxy, right belief and right action. Members commit to a "rule of life" much as monastics did. This rule describes the practices, relationships and experiences we commit ourselves to as those who participate in the community of Jesus known as Life Covenant Church. The rule represents the covenant we make to God and one another to live out Life's vision and values, and lists the practices that we find most important as a community. This includes participation in our three primary ministry structures (worship gatherings, expressions of community, and compassion and justice), as well as a commitment to practicing the spiritual disciplines, using our gifts to serve others, radical generosity and commitment to a lifestyle of friendship with those who are far from God. We see such a rule much as the Benedictines did, as a trellis that allows a plant to grow upward toward the sun even though it is not strong enough to support itself on its own.[33]

Small groups. Larry Crabb describes the small group experience of many when he relates the comments of one pastor: "We arrange our bodies in a circle, but our souls are sitting in straight-back chairs facing away from the others."[34] Though the challenge of truly connecting is a multifaceted one, one important aspect of this challenge is related to the type of small groups we choose to employ.

There seems to be two primary types of small groups that (with their variations) are fairly typical of churches. The first is the Bible study model. The primary goal in this small group is learning from the Scriptures, usually with an emphasis on life application.

This group is typically characterized by generous amounts of discussion of biblical texts (or perhaps a book on Christian living that is being studied) and wrestling with ideas. The primary strength of this model is a significant one: it helps people engage deeply with and be shaped by Scripture.

The second is the therapeutic model of small groups. The primary goal is listening to and helping one another in our walk with Christ. Typically this group is characterized by a generous amount of personal sharing and the development of a strong community environment. Life issues are discussed in depth, and help may be given to one another in the form of counsel, encouragement, prayer and accountability. The primary strength of this model is also significant: it can effectively connect believers in community as they seek to follow Christ in day-to-day life.

Our church has attempted a sort of hybrid, which we refer to as a missional small group. The primary goal of this model is to live as an expression of the kingdom of God. It is characterized by both study and fellowship, but both of these are understood and exercised within the context of mission. Great care is taken to be sure that our study of the Bible is not reduced to mere knowledge acquisition, and fellowship is never reduced to mere therapy. We desire these groups to function as missionary bands, studying the Bible together and ministering healing to one another as they embark on mission together. By maintaining a focus on mission, we hope to avoid what C. Peter Wagner calls "koinonitis," the inward-looking condition that comes when a local congregation has lost its purpose.

These groups are given three goals: to facilitate the spiritual formation of believers; to seek out, welcome and embrace those who are from God; and to serve together in ministries of compassion and justice. Within these parameters, each group has a different emphasis. Some practice spiritual disciplines together and spend time in lectio divina or some other form of meditation. Others are characterized by a zeal for serving others. Most spend a significant portion of their time in Scripture or a book they are reading together. One group watches films and discusses implications of each film for life and faith. These differing emphases are determined largely by the gifts of the leaders and the preferences of the group.

Two historical models have informed our approach to small groups. The first is the Celtic monastic communities. Monks in this tradition cultivated community with special care because they understood that a loving, grace-filled community was more than an important means of spiritual growth; it was a powerful evangelistic tool in a pagan culture. While monasteries in the East often formed as an escape from or protest against culture, Celtic monasticism was designed to "penetrate the pagan world and expand the church."[35]

When they evangelized Ireland, Celtic monks formed small monasteries and used them as bases of hospitality from which to reach out to the surrounding population. The Celtic apostolic teams engaged the local people in friendship and conversation, prayed for their needs, counseled people, healed the sick and interceded for the demon-possessed. St. Patrick was even known to pray blessings on the local rivers so that the people might catch more fish.[36]

Their model was developed in a pre-Christendom environment and is instructive for us as we minister in a post-Christendom environment. In Celtic evangelism, community, hospitality and serving the stranger were key components. Seekers were invited to belong before they believed. The circumstances of their conversions were not unlike those Robert Webber observes among postmoderns: "People come to faith not because they see the logic of the argument, but because they have experienced a welcoming God in a hospitable and loving community."[37]

John Wesley's class meeting is the second model that influences our approach. In Wesley's small group communities, ten to twelve men and women met weekly to study the Bible, pray for one another and help one another grow spiritually.[38] Wesley saw these groups as the heart of his movement.[39]

Wesley's class meetings placed great emphasis on the behavioral dimension of the faith, knowing that Christianity must be something lived and not merely believed. They were intentionally experiential and saw little value in groups that were merely cognitive. According to D. Michael Henderson, what set Wesley's groups apart was that, rather than telling people what they should do, Methodists were telling each other what they were actually doing.[40]

These groups were very effective in mission as well. More people came to faith through these groups than through Wesley's very successful preaching ministry. In addition, active concern for the poor was manifest in these groups. Each group member was required every week to bring a penny, which was used for care of the poor. Organizing his movement into such groups created 100 percent participation and mobilization into ministry.[41]

In addition to small groups, Life Covenant also encourages smaller gatherings of two or three people to meet for mentoring (a very important ministry at Life) or accountability with peers. These pairings or triads provide a very intimate level of fellowship, are an excellent venue in which to practice the disciplines of examination and confession, and aid in Scripture reading. The format is simple, generally consisting of a time of sharing what each person has been reading in the Scriptures, confession of sin and accountability, and prayer for one another.[42]

Dietrich Bonhoeffer pointedly observed that in a community where confession of sins is not taking place, only a thin veneer of fellowship can exist. Grace does not mark the community as it should because no one dares to be *real*. "The final break-through to fellowship does not occur, because, though they have fellow-

ship as devout people, they do not have fellowship as the unde-
vout, as sinners. The pious fellowship permits no one to be a sinner."[43] A church where confession is not practiced will have
shallow relationships and little sharpening of one another will
occur.

Such expressions of community help ground our lives not just
in the learning of the Scriptures but in the practice. It is said that
one early rabbi spoke of the feet, rather than the ears, as the primary body part for ingesting the Scriptures; we learn God as we
follow the Rabbi.[44] The Scriptures require our participation, not
just our observation.

Hospitality. For Jesus, the table was an important symbol of the
kingdom. Jesus modeled for his followers a radically inclusive table fellowship in which he regularly welcomed notorious sinners
and the ethnically and religiously unacceptable (Samaritans and
Gentiles) to become his friends. This practice was itself an embodied proclamation of the availability of the kingdom and the
opportunity to receive the friendship and mercy of God.[45]

This practice of inclusion clearly held both an evangelistic and
a formational dimension. Zacchaeus stands as an example of those
who were far from God but recognized in the meal God's invitation to them (Lk 19:1-10). By making his disciples a part of these
meals, Jesus also was instructing them in the ways of the kingdom. Jesus' followers would have understood that such inclusive
fellowship was to be their way of living as well.

There is also a connection between the table ministry of Jesus
and his ministry at the Last Supper. It is evident from the Gospels
that the disciples saw continuity between that final meal and others that Jesus had presided over. In the Upper Room as Jesus broke
bread and offered it to his followers, the words he used (*take, bless,
break* and *give*) were familiar ones. This same verbal formula is
recorded in all four Gospels at the feeding of the five thousand,
and in Matthew and Mark at the feeding of the four thousand.

Luke invokes it a final time in his Gospel as Jesus presides over supper with two disciples in Emmaus (Lk 24:30), and Paul also incorporates these words in his instructions on communion (1 Cor 11:23-24).[46] In offering his friendship at various tables, Jesus foreshadowed his offer of friendship represented at the communion Table and ultimately at the cross.

Jesus' first followers continued with his practice of hospitality and table fellowship. Romans 12:13 is representative of a familiar New Testament command: "Share with the Lord's people who are in need. Practice hospitality" (cf. 1 Pet 4:9; Heb 13:2; 3 Jn 1:8). Inclusion at one's table was apparently part of the normal Christian life for first-century believers, and regularly practicing hospitality was a requirement for both men and women who aspired to leadership (1 Tim 3:2; 5:10). "Eating," Robert Webber tells us, "has always played a central role in the Christian faith."[47]

At Life we want our ministry of hospitality to be rooted in an understanding of the enormous friendship of God. We want Jesus' capacity for welcoming the sinner and the stranger to spill over into our homes and be demonstrated around our dinner tables, even as it did for the early church. In a place like Los Angeles, where pace and lifestyle seem to magnify the distance between people, this ministry is very important.

Similarly, the postmodern generation's hunger for community creates a great opportunity for the gospel. Eddie Gibbs and Ryan Bolger identify hospitality as a central practice (as opposed to an optional extra) of emerging churches. These churches see hospitality as a two-sided coin: welcoming the stranger and serving the stranger.[48] Eugene Peterson also recognizes the centrality of hospitality: "When we realize how integral acts of hospitality are in evangelism, maybe we will be more deliberate and intentional about it."[49]

Our congregation eats together often. Since its first meetings in our living room, the church has made an effort to eat together every six to eight weeks. In addition to this, part of the hospitality ministry is to have families make a point of filling their tables with others from the church on a monthly basis. (My wife and I are included in this. We have made a goal of having the entire church over for dinner, four to six people at a time.) This simple ministry has been a key facet of assimilating newcomers into the church, as well as developing bonds between those in the church who might not naturally cross paths. With a little purposeful co-ordination, we have been able to utilize this ministry to introduce younger people to older ones, who eventually become their mentors, develop relationships that give a newcomer the courage to join a small group or to foster more meaningful social relationships within the body.

CONCLUSION

One aspect of an embodied apologetic, as we envision it, is that it is communal in nature. Being made in the image of the triune God, the desire for community is imprinted on our souls. For the people of God, community is a theological reality; we are deeply connected to one another as the result of our participation in the work of Christ. As we become a community of people who look more and more like Jesus, we begin to practice a communal apologetic. In our congregation we find certain ministry structures, including high-commitment membership, small groups and hospitality, to be especially helpful in cultivating this.

7

Enacted Faith

The Word became flesh and blood, and moved into the neighborhood.

JOHN 1:14 THE MESSAGE

What Thomas said of Christ, the world is saying about the church. . . .
"Unless I see in your hands the print of the nails, I will not believe."

JOHN STOTT, *THE CROSS OF CHRIST*

"Michelle lost her baby."

"What do you mean?" I heard myself say. It was two days before Michelle's due date, and my mind couldn't accept the possibility that she had had to endure delivering her precious baby stillborn. Michelle and her boyfriend, Lucky, worked at Starbucks, where we were beginning to become friends. She and my wife were pregnant at the same time, and each day when I came in for coffee we would compare notes on food cravings and aversions, who was how sick, and ultrasound pictures.

My friend on the other end of the phone continued, "She is asking for you, so I called all the Starbucks employees until I found someone with your number."

At the hospital I found Michelle in bed, her dad and boyfriend there to comfort her. We wept together, talked about and prayed to the God she didn't know if she believed in. The next week I led a graveside service for baby Hayley, with some of Michelle's family and friends in attendance, in a part of the cemetery reserved for children. When the service was over, Michelle hung her arms around my neck and sobbed. "Tim, I don't know what this means," she whispered, *"but I need God."*

Prior to this, I had been praying for Lucky and Michelle for months as we began to develop a friendship. They were a little wary of me as a pastor and made it clear they were not interested in church or talking about God. But the door to spiritual conversation began to open one day when I told them a story about our church's compassion work. Our congregation is deeply involved in issues of poverty and disease in Africa and our own city. They were surprised that a church would be so involved in real-world issues ("I thought you guys just kind of sat around and talked about what you believed and in what you are and aren't supposed to do") and were particularly fascinated by our work in Africa.

Our ministries of compassion and justice gave them a reason to listen and to begin to entertain the idea that there might be something good about Christianity. When their baby died and our church made them meals and sent them cards, they ended up being recipients of that compassion as well. "None of them have ever even met us," they said. "Why would they want to do this for us?"

If our witness is to be plausible in a postmodern world, our faith must be lived out in ways that show God's compassionate heart. It is not enough for us to talk about God's love for the world—we have to enact it. As we consider how to embed an enacted apologetic in the fabric of our congregations, our ministries of compassion and justice stand out as especially relevant. Along with worship gatherings and smaller expressions of community, our congregation has made compassion one of the three central ministries that we urge everyone to participate in, both for their own formation and as a place where they can involve friends who are far from God. In this chapter we will consider how these ministries might serve as an enacted apologetic.

COMPASSION AND JUSTICE IN THE MISSION OF GOD

Giving is at the heart of the gospel. The biblical record is the story of God giving himself to his people. Beginning with the opening lines of Genesis, we encounter a God who gives life, breath and sustenance to those he has created. As the New Testament opens, we see that in the incarnation, life, death and resurrection of Jesus, God gives not just his gifts but his very self for his people. Jesus came to give himself as the Lamb of God who would take away the sins of the world (Jn 1:29). He was the one and only Son of the Father, given to death on a cross that people might put their faith in him and find eternal life (Jn 3:14-16). Our own God served as "a ransom for all people" (1 Tim 2:6), that he might be both just and the one who justifies those who have placed their trust in him (Rom 3:26).

Our God gives himself away, and those who follow and are shaped into his image will become givers as well. Among other things, to be shaped into the image of Christ means we become increasingly other-centered. "Do nothing out of selfish ambition or vain conceit," Paul writes. "Rather, in humility value others above yourselves, not looking to your own interests but each of you to the interests of the others. In your relationships with one another, have the same attitude of mind Christ Jesus had" (Phil 2:3-5).

Scripture has much to say about God's heart toward issues of poverty and injustice. Broadly stated, we could summarize the biblical material as follows: God cares deeply about injustice, does something about it and much of what he chooses to do he does through his people. As Lesslie Newbigin reminds us, we are not elected for privilege but for service; to live not as exclusive beneficiaries of God's saving work but as bearers of this grace to the rest of the world.[1] This truth needs to be seen in a church that is focused outward, committing itself to the work of evangelism, compassion and justice on both a local and global scale.

Scripture portrays Yahweh as the world's rescuer and redeemer—one who steps into this situation to bring relief to the hurting and justice to the oppressed.

> Blessed are those whose help is the God of Jacob,
>   whose hope is in the LORD their God.
> He is the Maker of heaven and earth,
>   the sea, and everything in them—
>   he remains faithful forever.
> He upholds the cause of the oppressed
>   and gives food to the hungry.
> The LORD sets prisoners free,
>   the LORD gives sight to the blind,
> the LORD lifts up those who are bowed down,
>   the LORD loves the righteous.
> The LORD watches over the foreigner
>   and sustains the fatherless and the widow,
>   but he frustrates the ways of the wicked (Ps 146:5-9).

God not only brings justice to the oppressed, but he brings oppressors to justice. God is not dispassionate about injustice. Rather, he is a God "who takes sides, who gets angry, who knows right from wrong."[2]

> But you, God, see the trouble of the afflicted;
>   you consider their grief and take it in hand.
> The victims commit themselves to you;
>   you are the helper of the fatherless.
> Break the arms of the wicked and the evildoers;
>   call them to account for their wickedness
>   that would not otherwise be found out. . . .
> You, LORD, hear the desire of the afflicted;
>   you encourage them, and you listen to their cry,
> defending the fatherless and the oppressed,
>   so that mere earthly mortals
>   will never again strike terror. (Ps 10:14-15, 17-18)

Through the prophet Micah, God declares that he requires his people "to act justly and to love mercy / and to walk humbly with your God" (Micah 6:8).

When we neglect this we fall short of the biblical understanding of righteousness. Some of the harshest critiques that the Old Testament prophets uttered were aimed at those who claim to worship God but neglect the poor and those suffering injustice. "I am sick of your sacrifices!" God cries through Isaiah. "I cannot stand the sight" of your worship, and will no longer listen to the prayers of those with blood on their hands. It's as if God is saying, "How can you claim to love me, when you don't love those I love?" Instead, he says,

Learn to do good.
　Seek justice.
Help the oppressed.
　Defend the cause of orphans.
　Fight for the rights of widows. (Is 1:17 NLT)

Jesus seizes on this language when he rebukes the Pharisees for being so meticulous in giving that they tithe from their herb gardens, yet they neglect "the more important matters of the law—justice, mercy and faithfulness" (Mt 23:23). Righteousness that does not result in care for God's beloved is not righteousness at all.

From Eden onward, God has made clear his intentions to redeem the world and undo the damage that the Fall has wreaked on his creation (Gen 3:15). The biblical narrative tells of God's concern for his people and his intervention on their behalf. God acts as the world's savior, restoring what fallen humanity never could. For now, suffering is permitted (though God often intervenes), and eventually suffering will altogether cease when God's kingdom is fully ushered in (1 Cor 15:24; Rev 21:4).

Since the church now serves as a sign, instrument and the

world's first taste of God's in-breaking kingdom, its mission must reflect God's heart for the world. In addition to evangelism, this means joining God in his work of compassion and justice.

Compassionate Service as Enacted Apologetic

"Where are the hidden cameras?" was the best line of the night. Our congregation participates in a ministry called "Laundry Love," where on a given night we take over a local laundromat and our church does laundry for the homeless and working poor in our city.[3] It's a great opportunity to hear people's stories, laugh together and pray for our new friends while clothes are soaking and spinning. One man showed up not knowing we would be paying for his laundry and broke into tears. "This helps so much," he said. He had new twins at home, and he didn't know how they could afford them. Shawn and Melissa, a homeless couple we met through the dinners we host for the homeless in our city and who recently began attending our church, now consider Laundry Love their ministry too. They come and do their clothes, but come to serve others too.

Eugene Peterson astutely observes that, in North America, our primary method of bearing witness to the cross of Christ is verbal. We have little room in our understanding for incarnational action constituting evangelism.

> [Evangelism] is carried out among us primarily by saying something. Such witness and preaching is commonly detached from a local context that is textured with ongoing personal relationships. . . . The language is largely formulaic, dominated by the rhetoric of advertising and public relations. This is a language suitable for crowds and strangers but of dubious usefulness in conveying anything personal, and Jesus' work of salvation is nothing if not personal.[4]

Verbal witness is essential, but in a postmodern society dominated by skepticism and distrust, something more is needed, often before a verbal proclamation is given. Actions precede words. The pragmatic does-this-work spirit of our culture requires that our faith demonstrate its ability to make a difference in the world if it is to be considered at all.

In addition to this tendency to judge the truth of a faith by what it produces, the postmodern generations are longing for purpose, and are eager to give their lives to causes that will change the world. An apologetic that is enacted speaks to this longing. As Gibbs and Bolger put it, "Those outside the faith are more interested in the ethics of Christians than their doctrines."[5]

As intimidating as this can be, it is a challenge that the church should embrace. If we are indeed apprentices of Jesus, then we are well-suited to respond. We need only to follow the example of our Master. Erwin McManus rightly notes, "For too long we have hidden behind the rightness of propositional truth and have ignored the question of whether or not [our faith] works."[6]

In the Gospels and early church. Such an approach is well-supported by the Scriptures and finds many concrete examples in the history of the church. Perhaps more than anywhere else, we see this emphasis in the life of Jesus. His verbal proclamation of the kingdom is consistently accompanied by a demonstration of the kingdom. As John the Baptist languished in prison and wondered whether Jesus is indeed the Messiah, Jesus offered his miracles and acts of kindness as proofs: the hungry were fed, the sick made well, the demonized delivered, "good news . . . proclaimed to the poor" (Mt 11:4-5), and the people "were all amazed at the greatness of God" (Lk 9:43). The works of Jesus accompany and bear witness to his words. At the pivot point of history, as God took on flesh and brought about the redemption of the world, we find God "liberating the poor and oppressed and summoning his people to do the same."[7]

The book of Acts also contains many examples of the good works of the church acting as an apologetic for its message. In Acts 3–6 one sees the growth of the church in Jerusalem tied closely to the way that the faith is enacted. The public healing of a beggar, the regular and selfless sharing of financial resources, and the distribution of food to widows all contributed to the rapid spread of the church, and even a "large number of priests became obedient to the faith" (Acts 6:7). The believing community, as they were being transformed by Christ, was attractive to those around them. Their faith was not relegated to the realm of "religion" but reached into every corner of life, even their economic practices. The church's efforts and resources were directed toward "the least of these," and consequently the gospel was taken seriously by its hearers.

As the gospel spread beyond Jerusalem into more pluralistic societies, it is evident that such compassion continued to be the regular practice of the church. Collections were taken from the churches in Asia Minor to care for the even poorer believers in Judea (see Rom 15:26-28; 1 Cor 16:1-4; 2 Cor 8–9). Care for the poor and widows is praised as exemplary in the local church (Acts 9:36). In his farewell to the Ephesian elders, Paul reminds them both of his own example and of Christ's teaching: "In everything I did, I showed you that by this kind of hard work we must help the weak, remembering the words the Lord Jesus himself said: 'It is more blessed to give than to receive'" (Acts 20:35). Paul also notes that at the Jerusalem council nothing was added to his message, but the elders asked only that the churches continue to serve the poor (Gal 2:10).

Care for widows who could not care for themselves was normal Christian practice (1 Tim 5:3-10), and James describes pure religion as taking care of the helpless: "to look after orphans and widows in their distress and to keep oneself from being polluted by the world" (Jas 1:27). Paul assures the church at Corinth that the result of their compassionate service will be glory given to God: "People will praise God for the obedience that accompanies your confession of the gospel of Christ, and for your generosity in sharing with them" (2 Cor 9:13). This is an enacted apologetic that accompanies and incarnates the gospel message.

There is evidence of this kind of apologetic beyond the first century as well. A wildly loving community of faith is the explanation scholars see for the rapid spread of Christianity in its early centuries. As late as the fourth century we find Emperor Julian, despairing at the rise of Christianity and decline of paganism, writing to his high priest in Galatia:

> Why do we not observe that it is [the Christian's] benevolence to strangers, their care for the graves of the dead and the pretended holiness of their lives that have done the most to increase [Christianity]? . . . When . . . the impious Galileans support not only their own poor, but ours as well, all men see that our people lack aid from us.[8]

In the twenty-first century. A faith community that looks like Jesus is itself a powerful, enacted apologetic. Like the world of the early Christians, ours is a highly pluralistic society. The postmodern generations need to see our faith embodied if they are to accept the claims of Christ. Jesus' followers are meant to follow in his steps, trusting that as we serve, people will see God's heart in our actions and praise our Father in heaven (Mt 5:13-16).

The evangelistic function of compassionate ministry is much like that of worship: evangelism comes as a byproduct. Good compassion is good evangelism. In fact, our evangelism is not as much to those we are serving as to those we bring with us. Evangelism happens as we allow our non-Christian friends to see and participate in the life of the Christian community. Worship and small group study held no interest for a number of people in our church, but a friend's invitation to swing a hammer at a Habitat for Hu-

manity site or to help at a homeless dinner—these struck a chord
and resonated in that part of their souls that knows they were
made for a purpose.

I was walking with my family in the park one hot day when I
was approached by some Christians handing out bottles of water.
I had water already so I said no thank you and kept walking. But
to my surprise they followed me! I kept refusing but they kept at
it, asking if I was sure, pointing out the heat, reminding me I'd
probably get thirsty eventually. I finally took it, just so the stalk-
ing would stop. A small card with a map to their church was attached to the bottle. My wife looked at me and said, "Wow. If we
weren't already Christians that sure *wouldn't* have helped us get
there."

To have an apologetic function, our compassion ministries
must not have a hidden agenda. While our earnest hope is always
that those we serve might come to know Jesus, we have to make
sure our efforts aren't just another kind of bait-and-switch ploy.
Compassionate service is worthy in and of itself as a part of God's
kingdom mission, and does not need the presence of an evangelistic message to validate it.

If we are going to serve in this way, it must truly be that—service, with no expectation of receiving any particular result. Those
in the media-savvy crap-detector generation have grown up with
countless sales pitches and will not be taken in by those who do
not live out their message. "In contrast to a salesperson, a servant
does not present a product but gives himself or herself."[9]

Compassionate acts come out of hearts of compassion. If we are
to enact our apologetic, these acts of compassion cannot be programs that come and go, but must become part of the fabric of the
church—the stuff of the everyday lives of our people.

As spiritual formation. We're reminded once again of the importance of spiritual formation. For the faith community to serve
as an embodied apologetic, it must be a community of people who

are being transformed. Reasons to believe "will be offered most convincingly by those whose lives demonstrate the vitality of their message."[10]

As Christopher Wright points out, "I may wonder what kind of mission God has for *me*, when I should ask what kind of me God wants for *his* mission."[11]

And while this of course means helping our people pursue spiritual disciplines, we dare not underestimate the shaping power of compassionate ministry as a discipline itself. Too often we approach spiritual formation as entirely contemplative or intellectual, and forget the tremendous benefit we receive in serving others. Doug Pagitt captures this: "We're committed to living lives of service because of its formative qualities. Service isn't how we act out our spirituality; it's how our spirituality gets shaped."[12] How many in our churches, I wonder, are immature, not for lack of biblical knowledge but for lack of obedience to Christ's command to serve those in need?

As we reach out to others in need, we find that our compassion expands, and consequently so does our capacity to receive and give away God's grace. The compassionate life corrects warped perspectives of ourselves and our struggles, allowing us to see ourselves properly. On the one hand, in serving those who are needier than we are, it reminds us of our own need—that life is a gift and that all we have and are comes from God's hand. It reminds us that we are not as self-sufficient as we like to think, and that differing life circumstances could easily put us in a place of desperate need as well. Through compassionate service we learn humility.

On the other hand, engaging in compassionate service reminds us that we have something to give. Whatever resources we have received are not for our benefit alone but for the good of the world around us. The compassionate life develops in us an appropriate selflessness. As we bring together these two aspects of receiving and giving grace, God shapes in us a proper perspective of ourselves as servants. We are not the rescuers of the needy but recipients of God's grace, co-opted as his fellow workers to bring that grace to others.

Compassionate service also shapes us in our relationship with our money. Materialism and the related sins of greed and envy are very American sins, and for that reason they often go unrecognized in our lives. Despite our relative wealth (globally speaking) and abundance of possessions, Americans have a difficult time feeling they have enough. In what has been termed "affluenza," the unceasing quest for more is a cultural value that goes largely unquestioned in society or the church. Cultural observers Craig Detweiler and Barry Taylor, commenting on the pervasiveness of materialism, note, "While we've been arguing about sex and violence, television has been quietly teaching our children that the purpose of life is to shop."[13]

Being rich is not sinful, nor is being poor virtuous. Scripture portrays the *love* of money, not money itself, as the root of all kinds of evil (1 Tim 6:10). When the wealthy are condemned, it is not for being wealthy but for either gaining wealth by oppressing the poor or failure to share their resources with the needy. With money comes the power to enhance our life, bless others and to be used for the good of God's kingdom (Lk 16:9; 1 Tim 6:17-18).

At the same time, we must not treat money as if it is neutral. Money has more power over us than we realize. Jesus describes it as a god that vies for our affection (Mt 6:24), and he warns us that we cannot serve both it and God. Similarly, Paul warns that "those who want to get rich fall into temptation and a trap and into many foolish and harmful desires that plunge people into ruin and destruction" (1 Tim 6:9). In his intensive study of global Christianity, Philip Jenkins observes, "Christianity is flourishing wonderfully among the poor and persecuted, while it atrophies among the rich and secure."[14] Could this be due in part to our inattention to Scripture's warnings of money's power to keep us from God?

The ancients recognized that certain spiritual disciplines help us relate properly to our money and material possessions. The disciplines of simplicity and generosity historically have been used by God's people to keep money from occupying an improper place in our hearts. In choosing to live on less than we could, not cluttering our lives with an excess of material possessions, and giving our money away, we find that money loses its power over us.[15] Along with these, God's people have also recognized compassionate service as a spiritual discipline. It functions as a discipline by exposing us to the needy, reminding us that God is the source of our plenty and calling us to sacrifice on behalf of others.

As a society, twenty-first-century Americans are the most affluent people to ever walk the earth. This is not an accident of history, nor is it something to feel guilty about. For Christians in America, it is simply part of what it means to be the church at this junction in history, and we need to accept the responsibilities that come with that call.

On a corporate level, making compassionate service one of the primary ministries of the church keeps the church focused outward. When ministry serves only the needs of those within the body, a type of ecclesial entropy pulls the church away from being a "go to them" church and toward being a "come to us" church. Ministry to those within the church is an essential aspect of building authentic community, but if it exists without a missional focus, it becomes unhealthy. To maintain balance we need both inward ministry and outward mission. "Mission without ministry can lead to imperialism. Ministry without mission can become narcissism."[16] Practicing compassionate service helps us avoid these extremes.

EVANGELISM OR SOCIAL ACTION?

In recent history the relationship between evangelism and social action has been an awkward one. For the first half of the twentieth century, a debate raged in the church over whether evangelism or social action was the more faithful embodiment of God's mission. The battle resulted with the liberal wing of the church claiming social action and the conservative wing claiming evangelism. Healing this dichotomy was an explicit concern of those who launched the neo-evangelical movement in the middle of the century. Carl F. H. Henry, who in the founding of neo-evangelicalism sought to bring these two forms of mission back together, liked to say that God is simultaneously "the God of justice and justification."[17] Yet in spite of this, social action has struggled to find its place in conservative churches.

Scripture makes it clear, however, that both of these activities are critical in God's mission (and consequently in the mission of the church). God's heart breaks over not only the eternal destiny of lost people but also the suffering and injustices that people endure in this life. Paying attention to one at the expense of the other is to deny the fundamental worth and dignity of human beings made in God's image. "Offering salvation for the soul alone and promising peace and justice only in the life to come is to abandon Christ in this world while hoping to be with him in the next."[18] God's mission is not merely to disembodied souls but to whole people.

When we look further back in church history we find that in New Testament and post-New Testament times both evangelism and social action have been understood as the mission of God. Richard Foster identifies the social justice tradition (or "compassionate life") as one of the six great streams of Christian expression throughout church history.[19] From the care of widows in Acts 6 to the early church caring for the sick at their own peril, to the various medieval orders dedicated to caring for the poor, to John Woolman's gentle but persistent fight against slavery, to William and Catherine Booth of the Salvation Army, care for the "least of these" has characterized the people of God as their faith is moved to concrete action.[20]

It is widely recognized among historians that many of the social triumphs of the nineteenth and twentieth centuries came through the church. The abolition of slavery, opposition to forced prostitution, prison reform, child labor reform, the building of hospitals and schools for the poor, care for the mentally ill, gains in women's rights, and the American Civil Rights Movement came at the hands of evangelical Christians. Increasingly the modern evangelical church is embracing this emphasis on ministering to the whole person. This is especially evident in those churches ministering to postmoderns, where compassionate service is seen as a defining characteristic of emerging churches.

Many churches struggle to live out social action when evangelism, with its eternal ramifications, seems it should be the church's priority. Other churches struggle with how to allow both evangelism and social action to be a robust part of their mission without either one eclipsing the other. Christopher Wright offers a helpful model when he speaks of the *ultimacy* rather than the *primacy* of evangelism. Without devaluing evangelism, Wright points out that a problem arises when we speak of evangelism as our priority. *Priority* implies that an activity is most important and should be our starting point, while in reality this is not always possible or practical, nor does it reflect the ministry of Jesus.

Instead, Wright prefers to talk about the *ultimacy* of evangelism. If we keep in mind that God's mission is to the whole person and look at the whole circle of intertwined needs a person or community has (physical, mental, spiritual, social), we can enter this circle at any point of need. Priority is not necessarily given to spiritual need, as in a given case another need may be more pressing or make more sense as an entry point. Yet at the same time, to be faithful we must eventually make our way around the circle to evangelism. "Mission may not always *begin* with evangelism. But mission that does not ultimately *include* declaring the Word and the name of Christ, the call to repentance, and faith and obedience has not completed its task. It is defective mission, not holistic mission."[21]

GIVING SHAPE TO OUR COMPASSION

We believe that when we pray "Your kingdom come, your will be done, on earth as it is in heaven," a responsibility falls on us to do our part to make this prayer a reality. Part of living that prayer is a commitment to the compassionate life.

But if we are to see an enacted apologetic embedded in the life of the church, it needs to be more than a stated value. We need to take the additional step of providing specific ministry structures that can serve as vehicles for this value to be lived out. Our goal at Life is to provide multiple vehicles, both locally and globally, to enable us to carry out this aspect of our discipleship to Jesus.

Local. Twenty minutes away from us is Los Angeles's Skid Row, where legions of homeless people live and dozens of rescue missions and ministries operate. But in our ministries of compassion we have chosen to minister in our own city as much as we can. We do this for a couple of reasons. First, we want compassion to be part of what the normal Christian life looks like, and not something that is only practiced on "field trips." Our city definitely has a suburban, middle-class feel to it, but like almost every city, it has its homeless and working poor. Engaging in mission elsewhere is valuable too, but we don't want our people to disconnect compassion from their own neighborhoods. Second, since our compassionate service is an important part of our apologetic, we want the community God has placed our church in to see, hear and feel the benefits of his work through us in their midst.

We have a number of initiatives that we feel are a good fit for our community. We have an important ministry to the homeless and working poor. We partner with other churches to host a weekly dinner where our friends are able to get a hot, healthy meal and linger in a warm environment. I love watching our people (and the friends they bring) walking around refilling milk glasses, sitting and chatting, hearing stories, and offering whatever they have to give. Nurses from our church offer counsel and minor treatment, one young lady gives manicures to our friends, and others offer prayer or sack lunches to go. The dinner is often paired with a donation drive to meet some need that month as well (socks, blankets, toiletries, etc.). Every other month we do our laundry ministry as well, which is another great place to cultivate these relationships.

Our community places a very high value on education and prides itself in having an outstanding, though typically under-funded, school system. This led a handful of churches to come together for an annual work day to serve the community under the banner of a new organization called ShareFest. In the schools and elsewhere we paint, clean, landscape, erase graffiti, plant trees, pick up trash, beautify parks, do home repairs for the elderly, re-store historic sites and do other simple acts of kindness.

In five years ShareFest grew from the fifteen or so founding churches to include more than fifty, as well as an additional fifty or more PTAs and other outside groups. On our last work day in 2009 more than 8,000 volunteers were mobilized to complete 225 projects in our community. City governments and school officials that at first viewed us with skepticism now call to make sure their particular project will make it onto the list. Several city mayors and our State Representative have presented ShareFest with hon-ors, and deeply appreciate the churches' service to the city.

Our church serves in similar ways on an ongoing basis through our Do! Team. This group's ministry is to come to the aid of those in the congregation (and more so for friends and neighbors of those in the congregation) and help people move, make home re-pairs, paint, clean, babysit and so forth. Their goal is simply to meet physical needs as an expression of Christ's love.

Many other ministries of compassion happen at Life on a more sporadic basis. We have a partnership with an orphanage in Mexico that we work at annually, and this year we were able to provide Christmas gifts for all of their kids as well. On occasion congregants (often in small groups) have served with Habitat for Humanity, a local battered-women's shelter, and ran or biked to raise money to serve the poor or oppressed.

It is a joy for our church to watch our church plants prayerfully serve their communities' needs as well. Restoration Covenant Church is located in Redlands, California, where they have been active in caring for HIV/AIDS patients and children in homes where a parent is infected. They have also formed a partnership with local law enforcement, providing hygiene kits with new undergarments for rape victims who are brought to the police station or hospital.

Global. Knowing that we were going to be a smaller church with limited resources shaped the global strategy we adopted. We opted for a laser beam rather than a shotgun approach, deciding we would prayerfully select one region in the world and minister there for twenty years. Our hope is that in doing this we can have a deeper impact than we could with a more hit-and-run approach to mission, and develop real relationships with the locals that we are empowering through our work.

Two priorities guided us as we selected a location: we wanted to serve a largely unreached area, and we felt a deep responsibility to minister in the midst of the crushing poverty and AIDS pandemic that grips sub-Saharan Africa. The intersection of those priorities landed us in Mozambique.

Two summers ago I served with a team from our congregation in Mozambique. There, 85 to 90 percent of the population lives on less than a dollar per day, and 70 percent of the adult population is unemployed. I will never forget the faces of Mozambican children I played with at a wonderfully rambunctious school run by missionaries. I asked the administrator if the children received any food assistance from the government. "Oh no," she said. "These children are considered well-fed. They eat one meal per day." In this part of the world, starvation and malnutrition are not theoretical but are very real issues they face on a daily basis.

Unfortunately this situation is not unique in our world. Tremendous needs exist both locally and globally, but are seen most dramatically in looking at the global picture. When we consider world hunger, approximately one billion people currently live at the most extreme level of poverty, subsisting on one dollar or less per day. An additional 1.6 billion people, considered moderately poor, live on between one and two dollars per day.[22] For these people, daily survival is a struggle.

Such extreme poverty goes hand-in-hand with disease. Disease is both a cause and a result of poverty. The lack of national wealth means there is very little health care, and the absence of such care creates an environment where the working population is increasingly decimated by disease, furthering the vicious cycle. Worldwide, nearly forty million people are infected with HIV/AIDS, 64 percent of whom are in Africa.[23] Amazingly, malaria takes even more lives in Africa than does AIDS. In all, fifteen thousand people per day die in Africa of AIDS, malaria and tuberculosis.[24] All three of these diseases are largely preventable or treatable.

Poverty causes more poverty. Below a certain level, all of a person's income goes toward day-to-day survival, with no reserve to put toward bettering his or her situation. Entire countries fail to thrive because this situation affords no opportunity for families to educate their children, save money, seek healthcare or employ better technology for farming or industry. Consequently, governments are not able to collect taxes to construct the roads and ports needed to facilitate trade and begin turning the economic situation around. This "poverty trap" creates a vicious downward spiral that is nearly impossible to break without outside assistance. In such settings, there is often little protection for the poor, who are subject to a dizzying array of additional injustices, from forced child labor to the threat of human trafficking.[25]

One of the most effective tools for combating deep poverty is microenterprise development. For five years now we have partnered with Opportunity International, a renowned pioneer in microfinance lending. Microenterprise works by providing very small loans (usually $75 to $200) to the poorest of the poor (typically AIDS widows). These women apply for this money as start-up capital for businesses they want to launch. These businesses include such ventures as raising chickens (to sell eggs), selling fruit, opening a grocery stand, making jewelry, sewing, basket weaving or starting a simple phone bank.

In addition to providing the microloan, Opportunity trains its clients in how to run a business, HIV/AIDS awareness and treatment, the importance of education (to break the cycle of poverty before it is passed on to the next generation), and spiritual support and nurture. The women are part of what is called a Trust Group, which co-guarantees each other's loans and supports their business ventures. Opportunity's success rate (as determined by the business providing income and the loan being repaid) is nearly 98 percent, making it one of the most effective means available for helping the poor. Rather than just feeding them for a day, Opportunity enables their clients to have an ongoing means of income and to do so with dignity and real hope for a better future.

Our church has enthusiastically embraced this ministry and has sacrificed to fund projects in Mozambique. To date, Life's resources have provided the means for nearly two thousand families to come out of the deepest level of poverty. I had the privilege of meeting some of these families while I was there, and I can hardly describe the joy I felt to see them holding their heads high (in a country where no one does), providing for their families, adopting and caring for the AIDS orphans in their communities, and in some cases giving work to others as their businesses expanded.

CONCLUSION

John Burke observes that one of the primary questions postmoderns ask is, "Do I want to be like you?"[26] They see truth as relational, and our faith appeals to them only as it reveals a God who is real and active in our lives and in the world. Living out God's compassion is part of embodying our apologetic, and it gives them reason to answer yes to that question.

In the same way, as we prayerfully engage in worship and nurture authentic community in our churches, we not only are formed as apprentices of Jesus but also find an opportunity to embody our apologetic and allow those around us to "taste and see that the Lord is good." May God use our humble efforts to his glory.

Notes

Introduction

[1]David Fitch, *The Great Giveaway* (Grand Rapids: Baker, 2005), p. 29.

[2]A local church conducted a study that showed the likely number of people actively involved in churches in this area was likely less than 10 percent. This finding was based in part on attendance figures as well as the realization that there were not enough seats in all the local churches combined to hold even 10 percent of the South Bay of Los Angeles's nearly 900,000 residents.

[3]David Kinnaman and Gabe Lyons, *Unchristian* (Grand Rapids: Baker, 2007), p. 27.

[4]Ibid., pp. 31-32.

[5]Wade Clark Roof, *Spiritual Marketplace: Baby Boomers and the Remaking of American Religion* (Princeton, N.J.: Princeton University Press, 1999), p. 53.

[6]Tom Beaudoin, *Virtual Faith* (San Francisco: Jossey-Bass, 1998), p. 13.

[7]Kinnaman and Lyons, *Unchristian*, p. 74.

[8]Leonard Sweet, *Carpe Mañana* (Grand Rapids: Zondervan, 2001), p. 145.

[9]Jerry Adler, "In Search of the Spiritual," *Newsweek (online edition)* August 29–September 5, 2005, p. 1, accessed June 19, 2009, at <www.newsweek.com/id/147035>.

[10]Craig Detweiler and Barry Taylor, *A Matrix of Meanings* (Grand Rapids: Baker, 2003), p. 56.

[11]David T. Olson, *The American Church in Crisis* (Grand Rapids: Zondervan 2008). For more specific data on church attendance in a particular region or metropolitan area, visit <www.theamericanchurch.org>.

[12]Ibid., 26-29.

[13]Ibid., p. 28

[14]Ibid., p. 120.

[15]Ibid., p. 175.

[16]Philip Jenkins, *The Next Christendom* (Oxford: Oxford University Press, 2002), p. 3.

[17]Sweet, *Carpe Mañana*, p. 145. See also Reggie McNeal, *The Present Future* (San Francisco: Jossey-Bass, 2003), p. 4.

[18]Sweet, *Carpe Mañana*, p. 145.

[19]Reggie McNeal, *The Present Future* (San Francisco: Jossey-Bass, 2003), p. 4.

[20]Eddie Gibbs and Ryan Bolger, *Emerging Churches* (Grand Rapids: Baker, 2005), p. 29.

[21]McNeal, *Present Future*, p. 4.

[22]Mike Regele, *Death of the Church* (Grand Rapids: Zondervan, 1995), p. 173.

[23]One amazing example of this kind of "parenting" of a young congregation happened

with my friend Eugene Cho and Quest in Seattle. See Eugene Cho, "Quest and Its Relationship with the Evangelical Covenant Church," in Fuller Seminary's *Theology, News and Notes,* fall 2008 <http://documents.fuller.edu/news/pubs/tnn/2008_Fall/6_quest.asp>.

[24]McNeal, *Present Future,* p. 10.

[25]Stanley Grenz, *A Primer on Postmodernism* (Grand Rapids: Eerdmans, 1996), p. 40.

[26]Chuck Smith Jr., *The End of the World . . . As We Know It* (Colorado Springs: Waterbrook, 2001), pp. 35-41.

[27]Regele, *Death of the Church,* pp. 66-70.

[28]Eddie Gibbs, *ChurchNext* (Downers Grove, Ill.: InterVarsity Press, 2000), p. 20.

[29]John G. Stackhouse Jr., *Humble Apologetics* (New York: Oxford University Press, 2002), p. 22.

[30]Grenz, *Primer on Postmodernism,* p. 43.

[31]Ibid., p. 6.

[32]Ibid., pp. 148-50.

[33]Millard J. Erickson, *Truth or Consequences* (Downers Grove, Ill.: InterVarsity Press, 2001), p. 231.

[34]J. Richard Middleton and Brian J. Walsh, *Truth Is Stranger Than It Used to Be* (Downers Grove, Ill.: InterVarsity Press, 1995), p. 71.

[35]Millard J. Erickson, Paul Kjoss Helseth and Justin Taylor, eds., *Reclaiming the Center* (Wheaton, Ill.: Crossway, 2004), pp. 307-10.

[36]Smith, *End of the World,* 155.

[37]Stackhouse, *Humble Apologetics,* p. 5.

[38]Ibid., p. 60.

[39]See Lesslie Newbigin, *The Gospel in a Pluralist Society* (Grand Rapids: Eerdmans, 1989), p. 168.

[40]Erwin Raphael McManus, *An Unstoppable Force* (Loveland, Colo.: Group, 2002), p. 29.

[41]Beaudoin, *Virtual Faith,* pp. 37-47. See also Gibbs, *ChurchNext,* pp. 123-26.

[42]Gibbs, *ChurchNext,* p. 11.

[43]Beaudoin, *Virtual Faith,* p. 74.

[44]Christopher J. H. Wright, *The Mission of God* (Downers Grove, Ill.: InterVarsity Press, 2006), pp. 47-48.

Chapter 1: Show and Tell

[1]Millard J. Erickson, *Postmodernizing the Faith* (Grand Rapids: Baker, 1998), p. 152.

[2]Leonard Sweet, *AquaChurch* (Loveland, Colo.: Group, 1999), p. 29.

[3]Robert Webber, *The Younger Evangelicals* (Grand Rapids: Baker, 2002), p. 95.

[4]Curtis Chang, *Engaging Unbelief* (Downers Grove, Ill.: InterVarsity Press, 2000), p. 49.

[5]Erwin Raphael McManus, *An Unstoppable Force* (Loveland, Colo.: Group, 2002), p. 80. See also Rodney Clapp, *A Peculiar People* (Downers Grove, Ill.: InterVarsity Press, 1996), pp. 132-37.

[6]John G. Stackhouse Jr., *Humble Apologetics* (New York: Oxford University Press, 2002), p. 12.

[7]Craig Detweiler and Barry Taylor, *A Matrix of Meanings* (Grand Rapids: Baker, 2003), p. 85.

[8]Chang, *Engaging Unbelief*, p. 24.

[9]Webber, *Younger Evangelicals*, pp. 56, 126.

[10]My current favorite apologetic is Timothy Keller's *The Reason for God* (New York: Dutton, 2007). It offers a truly impressive blend of reason and passion, and speaks meaningfully to the questions unbelievers are asking.

[11]See for example William Lane Craig, "God Is Not Dead Yet," *Christianity Today*, July 2008, pp. 22-27. It is worth noting, however, that much of the case made by the new atheists is based on the gap between what the church says it believes and the way it actually lives. An embodied apologetic speaks to this gap in a way that rational apologetics alone do not.

[12]Stackhouse, *Humble Apologetics*, pp. 24-26.

[13]Webber, *Younger Evangelicals*, p. 84.

[14]Millard J. Erickson, *Truth or Consequences* (Downers Grove, Ill.: InterVarsity Press, 2001), p. 226.

[15]Richard F. Flory and Donald E. Miller, eds., *Gen X Religion* (New York: Routledge, 2000), p. 241.

[16]Stackhouse, *Humble Apologetics*, p. 228. Compare Millard Erickson, Paul Kjoss Helstethm, and Justin Taylor, eds., *Reclaiming the Center* (Wheaton, Ill.: Crossway, 2004), p. 335.

[17]John Calvin, *Institutes of the Christian Religion* (Grand Rapids: Eerdmans, 1962), 2:7, 1:505.

[18]Stackhouse, *Humble Apologetics*, p. 104.

[19]Ibid. Cf. Erickson, *Truth or Consequences*, pp. 260-64; Erickson, Helseth and Taylor, eds., *Reclaiming the Center*, p. 90.

[20]N. T. Wright, *The New Testament and the People of God* (Minneapolis: Augsburg Fortress, 1996), p. 35. For an accessible volume that offers arguments for and against foundationalist and postfoundationalist epistemologies, see Myron B. Penner, ed., *Truth and the Postmodern Turn* (Grand Rapids: Brazos, 2005).

[21]Philip D. Kenneson, "There's No Such Thing as Objective Truth, and It's a Good Thing, Too," *Christian Apologetics in the Postmodern World*, ed. Timothy R. Phillips and Dennis L. Ockholm (Downers Grove, Ill.: InterVarsity Press, 1995), p. 166.

[22]Stackhouse, *Humble Apologetics*, p. 38.

[23]Erwin Raphael McManus, *The Barbarian Way* (Nashville: Nelson, 2005), p. 61. See also Glen A. Scorgie, "Hermeneutics and the Case for a Baptized Imagination," *Journal of the Evangelical Theological Society* 44 (2001): 271-84.

[24]John Teter has pioneered an evangelism strategy around these seven signs. See John Teter, *Get the Word Out* (Downers Grove, Ill.: InterVarsity Press, 2003), p. 126.

[25]See also Acts 2; 3:9-10; 5:12-14; 8:6-8, 13; 9:20, 33-35, 42; 13:12; 16:26-32; 19:10-20.

[26]Gary M. Burge, *John*, NIV Application Commentary (Grand Rapids: Zondervan, 2000), p. 75.

[27]Webber, *Younger Evangelicals*, pp. 188-89.

[28]Ibid., p. 222.

[29]Doug Pagitt, *Reimagining Spiritual Formation* (Grand Rapids: Zondervan/Emergent YS, 2003), p. 27.

[30]Tertullian, quoted in Webber, *Younger Evangelicals*, p. 95.

[31]Webber, *Younger Evangelicals*, p. 130, emphasis in the original.

[32]McManus, *Barbarian Way*, p. 92.

[33]Dallas Willard, *Renovation of the Heart* (Colorado Springs: NavPress, 2002), p. 239.

[34]Lesslie Newbigin, *The Open Secret*, rev. ed. (Grand Rapids: Eerdmans, 1995), p. 110.

[35]Aristides, quoted in Brad Kallenberg, *Live to Tell: Evangelism in a Postmodern Age* (Grand Rapids: Brazos, 2002), pp. 53-54.

[36]David K. Clark, *Dialogical Apologetics* (Grand Rapids: Baker, 1993), p. 199.

[37]Brian D. McLaren, *A New Kind of Christian* (San Francisco: Jossey-Bass, 2001), p. 154.

Chapter 2: Same Wine, Different Skin

[1]Eddie Gibbs, *In Name Only* (Pasadena, Calif.: Fuller Seminary Press, 1994), p. 252.

[2]Lesslie Newbigin, *The Open Secret*, rev. ed. (Grand Rapids: Eerdmans, 1995), p. 2.

[3]I would contend, however, that the worship of God is not fully lived out if divorced from participation in God's mission. Just as we dare not separate our theology of church from our theology of mission, we dare not separate our theology of worship from our theology of mission.

[4]Darrell L. Guder, ed., *Missional Church* (Grand Rapids: Eerdmans, 1998), p. 84.

[5]Erwin Raphael McManus, *An Unstoppable Force* (Loveland, Colo.: Group, 2002), p. 30.

[6]Michael Frost and Alan Hirsch, *The Shaping of Things to Come* (Peabody, Mass.: Hendrickson, 2003), p. 83.

[7]Ajith Fernando, *Acts*, NIV Application Commentary (Grand Rapids: Zondervan, 1998), p. 480.

[8]Frost and Hirsch, *Shaping of Things to Come*, p. 83.

[9]Lesslie Newbigin, *The Gospel in a Pluralist Society* (Grand Rapids: Eerdmans, 1989), p. 144.

[10]Ron Martoia, *Morph* (Loveland, Colo.: Group, 2003), p. 17.

[11]Many commentators (dating as far back as Chrysostom) have suggested that Paul's hearers may have even mistakenly believed he was proclaiming two different gods: Jesus and Anastasis (the Greek word *anastasis* means "resurrection"). See Fernando, *Acts*, p. 474.

[12]Newbigin, *Open Secret*, p. 88.

[13]Tim Downs, *Finding Common Ground* (Chicago: Moody Press, 1999), p. 135.

[14]See Philip Jenkins, *The Next Christendom* (Oxford: Oxford University Press, 2002), p. 122.

[15]Newbigin, *Open Secret*, p. 186.

[16]The first quotation comes from the Cretan poet Epimenides' *Cretica* (c. 600 B.C.), and the second is from the Cicilian poet Aratus (c. 315-240 B.C.) in his *Phaenomena*, and is also found in Cleanthes' (331-233 B.C.) *Hymn to Zeus* (see Richard N. Longenecker, *Acts*, in *The Expositor's Bible Commentary*, ed. Frank Gaebelein, vol. 9, *John and Acts* [Grand Rapids: Zondervan, 1981], p. 476). See 1 Cor 15:33 and Tit 1:12 for other instances of Paul quoting Greek poets.

[17]Longenecker, *Acts*, p. 476.

[18]Curtis Chang, *Engaging Unbelief* (Downers Grove, Ill.: InterVarsity Press, 2000), pp. 26, 65.

[19]Tom Beaudoin, *Virtual Faith* (San Francisco: Jossey-Bass, 1998), p. 165.

[20]Chuck Smith Jr., *The End of the World . . . As We Know It* (Colorado Springs: Waterbrook, 2001), p. 193.

[21]Chang, *Engaging Unbelief*, p. 157.

[22]Smith, *End of the World*, p. 192.

[23]N. T. Wright, *The New Testament and the People of God* (Minneapolis: Augsburg Fortress, 1996), p. 279.

[24]Richard V. Peace, *Conversion in the New Testament* (Grand Rapids: Eerdmans, 1999), p. 288.

[25]It is notable that these now common methods encountered significant resistance as well. See Leonard Sweet, *AquaChurch* (Loveland, Colo.: Group, 1999), p. 183.

[26]Peace, *Conversion in the New Testament*, pp. 290-91.

[27]Eddie Gibbs, *ChurchNext* (Downers Grove, Ill.: InterVarsity Press, 2000), p. 211.

[28]See Brad J. Kallenberg, *Live To Tell* (Grand Rapids: Brazos, 2002), pp. 9-13.

[29]Frost and Hirsch, *Shaping of Things to Come*, p. 16.

[30]Michael Slaughter, *Unlearning Church* (Loveland, Colo.: Group, 2002), p. 51.

[31]Gibbs, *ChurchNext*, p. 148.

[32]Os Guinness, *Dining with the Devil* (Grand Rapids: Baker, 1993), pp. 28, 78.

[33]"The Epistle to Diognetus," in *The Apostolic Fathers*, ed. Michael W. Holmes, 2nd ed. (Grand Rapids: Baker, 1989), p. 299.

[34]George Hunter III, *The Celtic Way of Evangelism* (Nashville: Abingdon, 2000).

[35]David Jacobus Bosch, *Transforming Mission* (Maryknoll, N.Y.: Orbis, 1991), p. 449.

[36]Jenkins, *Next Christendom*, p. 32.

[37]Ibid., p. 36.

[38]George G. Hunter III, *Church for the Unchurched* (Nashville: Abingdon, 1996), p. 66.

[39]John Calvin, *Institutes of the Christian Religion* (Grand Rapids: Eerdmans, 1962), 2:182.

[40]Hunter, *Church for the Unchurched*, p. 66.

[41]Howard Taylor and Mrs. Howard Taylor, *Hudson Taylor's Spiritual Secret* (Chicago: Moody Press, 1989), pp. 64-74.

[42]C. S. Lewis, *God in the Dock* (Grand Rapids: Eerdmans, 1972), p. 338.

[43]Lesslie Newbigin, quoted in Ed Stetzer, *Planting New Churches in a Postmodern Age* (Nashville: Broadman & Holman, 2003), pp. 128-29.

⁴⁴This is illustrated in an interesting dialogue (*The Church in Emerging Culture: Five Perspectives*, ed. Leonard Sweet [Grand Rapids: Zondervan, 2003]) in which three very articulate authors contend for "low change" in methods in bringing the gospel to a postmodern culture. The arguments they raise are significant, but I can't help but notice that they represent three very different traditions (Reformed, Greek Orthodox and a multicultural parachurch experience). If we were to accept their premise that we shouldn't change our methods, we still must ask, Which of your traditions should we not change from?

⁴⁵Erwin McManus, "Past the Expiration Date," *The Church in Emerging Culture: Five Perspectives*, ed. Leonard Sweet (Grand Rapids: Zondervan, 2003), pp. 239-40.

⁴⁶Paul Hiebert, quoted in Frost and Hirsch, *Shaping of Things to Come*, pp. 89-94.

⁴⁷Ibid., p. 94.

⁴⁸Ibid., p. 90.

⁴⁹Ibid., p. 94.

Chapter 3: Living Out God's Mission in Disciplemaking

¹David Jacobus Bosch, *Transforming Mission* (Maryknoll, N.Y.: Orbis, 1991), p. 74.

²Dallas Willard, *The Great Omission* (San Francisco: HarperCollins, 2006), pp. 3-5.

³Michael Wilkins, *In His Image* (Colorado Springs: NavPress, 1997), p. 37.

⁴Richard V. Peace, *Conversion in the New Testament* (Grand Rapids: Eerdmans, 1999), p. 285.

⁵Ibid.

⁶Dan Kimball, *The Emerging Church* (Grand Rapids: Zondervan, 2003), p. 200.

⁷Scot McKnight, *Turning to Jesus* (Louisville: Westminster John Knox, 2002), p. 13.

⁸I am indebted to my friend Paul Kaak, who first got me thinking about disciplemaking in this way.

⁹Robert Webber, *Journey to Jesus* (Nashville: Abingdon, 2001), p. 11.

¹⁰Dave Olson, *The American Church in Crisis* (Grand Rapids: Zondervan 2008), pp. 167-68.

¹¹David Bosch, quoted in Darrell L. Guder, *The Continuing Conversion of the Church* (Grand Rapids: Eerdmans, 2000), p. 25.

¹²Scot McKnight, "Five Streams of the Emerging Church," *Christianity Today* 51, no. 2 (February 2007), accessed May 26, 2009, at <www.christianitytoday.com/ct/2007/february/11.35.html>.

¹³For a very helpful method, see Don Everts and Doug Schaupp, *I Once Was Lost* (Downers Grove, Ill.: InterVarsity Press, 2008).

¹⁴See Robert Webber, *Ancient-Future Evangelism* (Grand Rapids: Baker, 2003), p. 61.

¹⁵Doug Pagitt, *Reimagining Spiritual Formation* (Grand Rapids: Zondervan/Emergent YS, 2003), p. 117.

¹⁶Oswald Chambers, *My Utmost for His Highest* (Grand Rapids: Discovery House, 2006), October 17 entry.

¹⁷John G. Stackhouse Jr., *Humble Apologetics* (New York: Oxford University Press, 2002), p. ix.

Chapter 4: Disciplines of Disciples

[1]Dave Olson believes two growing edges in church planting are critical as we enter the twenty-first century—we need to plant churches that are intentional about reaching the growing multiethnic population, and churches that are intentional in reaching postmodern people (*The American Church in Crisis* [Grand Rapids: Zondervan 2008], pp. 152). See also Ed Stetzer, *Planting New Churches in a Postmodern Age* (Nashville: Broadman & Holman, 2003), pp. 3-11.

[2]Thomas Kelly, *A Testament of Devotion* (San Francisco: HarperCollins, 1941), p. 80.

[3]Ibid., pp. 19-20.

[4]Ray S. Anderson, *An Emergent Theology for Emerging Churches* (Downers Grove, Ill.: InterVarsity Press, 2006), p. 186.

[5]Dallas Willard, *Renovation of the Heart* (Colorado Springs: NavPress, 2002), p. 22.

[6]Ibid., p. 82.

[7]Ibid., p. 85.

[8]Thomas à Kempis, *The Imitation of Christ* (New York: Penguin, 1952), p. 139.

[9]Brother Lawrence, *The Practice of the Presence of God* (New Kensington, Penn.: Whitaker House, 1982), p. 90.

[10]James G. Lawson, *Deeper Experiences of Famous Christians* (New Kensington, Penn.: Whitaker House, 1998), p. 80.

[11]Dallas Willard, *The Divine Conspiracy* (San Francisco: HarperCollins, 1998), pp. 25-28.

[12]Darrell L. Guder, ed., *Missional Church* (Grand Rapids: Eerdmans, 1998), p. 101.

[13]C. S. Lewis, *The Weight of Glory and Other Addresses* (San Francisco: HarperCollins, 2001), p. 26.

[14]Willard, *Divine Conspiracy*, p. 93.

[15]David Jacobus Bosch, *Transforming Mission* (Maryknoll, N.Y.: Orbis, 1991), p. 66.

[16]William Law, *A Serious Call to a Devout and Holy Life* (Philadelphia: Westminster Press, 1948), p. 17 (emphasis added).

[17]Rodney Clapp, *A Peculiar People* (Downers Grove, Ill.: InterVarsity Press, 1996), p. 167.

[18]See Dallas Willard, *The Spirit of the Disciplines* (San Francisco: HarperCollins, 1991), pp. 156-57.

[19]Richard J. Foster, *Life with God* (San Francisco: HarperOne, 2008), pp. 15-18.

[20]Willard, *Spirit of the Disciplines*, p. 156.

[21]Richard J. Foster, *Celebration of Discipline*, rev. ed. (New York: Harper & Row, 1988).

[22]On breath prayers see Richard J. Foster, *Prayer* (San Francisco: HarperCollins, 1992), p. 122. On the daily examen see Dennis Linn, Sheila Fabricant Linn and Matthew Linn, *Sleeping with Bread* (Mahwah, N.J.: Paulist Press, 1995); see also Foster, *Prayer*, pp. 27-35. On spiritual direction see David Benner, *Sacred Companions: The Gift of Spiritual Friendship and Direction* (Downers Grove, Ill.: InterVarsity Press, 2004).

[23]Frank Laubach, "Games with Minutes," in *Man of Prayer* (Syracuse: Laubach Literacy International, 1990), p. 19.

[24]Foster, *Celebration of Discipline*, p. 8.

[25]Henri J. M. Nouwen, *The Way of the Heart* (New York: Ballantine, 1981), p. 13.

[26]Tarsicius Van Bavel, *The Rule of Saint Augustine* (Kalamazoo, Mich.: Cistercian, 1996), p. 3.

[27]Timothy Fry, ed., *The Rule of Saint Benedict* (New York: Vintage, 1998), p. xvi.

[28]George A. Lane, *Christian Spirituality* (Chicago: Loyola Press, 1984), p. 33.

[29]Ignatius of Loyola, *The Spiritual Exercises of St. Ignatius*, trans. Anthony Mattola (New York: Doubleday, 1989).

[30]Walter Trobisch, *Martin Luther's Quiet Time* (Downers Grove, Ill.: InterVarsity Press, 1975).

[31]John Calvin, *Institutes of the Christian Religion* (Grand Rapids: Eerdmans, 1962), 2:146.

[32]Jeremy Taylor, *The Rule and Exercises of Holy Living* (New York: Harper & Row, 1970).

[33]Two practical resources in teaching others to construct a rule of life are John Ortberg, *The Life You've Always Wanted* (Grand Rapids: Zondervan, 1997), pp. 189-204; and Ruth Haley Barton, *Sacred Rhythms* (Downers Grove, Ill.: InterVarsity Press, 2006), pp. 146-66.

[34]Ortberg, *Life You've Always Wanted*, p. 43.

[35]Law, *Serious Call to a Devout and Holy Life*, p. 7.

[36]Ortberg, *Life You've Always Wanted*, pp. 33-35.

[37]Dallas Willard, *Hearing God* (Downers Grove, Ill.: InterVarsity Press, 1999), p. 194.

[38]Foster, *Celebration of Discipline*, p. 9.

[39]Os Guinness, *Dining with the Devil* (Grand Rapids: Baker, 1993), p. 49.

[40]Brian McLaren, *More Ready Than You Realize* (Grand Rapids: Zondervan, 2002), p. 140.

[41]Brian McLaren, *A Generous Orthodoxy* (Grand Rapids: Zondervan, 2004), p. 260.

[42]Jimmy Long, *Generating Hope* (Downers Grove, Ill.: InterVarsity Press, 1997), p. 194.

[43]McLaren, *More Ready Than You Realize*, pp. 172-73.

[44]Graham Johnston, *Preaching to a Postmodern World* (Grand Rapids: Baker, 2001), p. 28.

[45]McLaren, *More Ready Than You Realize*, p. 52.

Chapter 5: Experiential Faith

[1]C. S. Lewis, *Letters to Malcolm: Chiefly on Prayer* (New York: Harcourt Brace, 1964), p. 103.

[2]Richard F. Flory and Donald E. Miller, eds., *Gen X Religion* (New York: Routledge, 2000), p. 8.

[3]See Sally Morgenthaler, *Worship Evangelism* (Grand Rapids: Zondervan, 1995), p. 81.

[4]Lewis, *Letters to Malcolm*, p. 4.

[5]I originally heard this metaphor at a seminar on worship led by Andy Crouch. I'm told that Lesslie Newbigin used it as well.

[6]Dan Kimball, *Emerging Church* (Grand Rapids: Zondervan, 2003), p. 115.

[7]Robert Webber, *The Younger Evangelicals* (Grand Rapids: Baker, 2002), p. 188.

[8]Ibid., p. 46.

[9]Wade Clark Roof, *Spiritual Marketplace* (Princeton, N.J.: Princeton University Press, 1999), p. 86.

[10]Chuck Smith Jr., *The End of the World . . . As We Know It* (Colorado Springs: Waterbrook, 2001), p. 91.

[11]Erwin Raphael McManus, *An Unstoppable Force* (Loveland, Colo.: Group, 2002), p. 177.

[12]Charles Kraft, quoted in Charles VanEngen, *God's Missionary People* (Grand Rapids: Baker, 1991), p. 116.

[13]Eugene Peterson, *Living the Resurrection* (Colorado Springs: NavPress, 2006), pp. 14-23.

[14]Robert Webber, *Ancient-Future Faith* (Grand Rapids: Baker, 1999), p. 29.

[15]Ibid.

[16]Ibid., p. 16.

[17]Ibid.

[18]Ibid., pp. 92-96.

[19]Ibid., p. 122.

[20]Smith, *End of the World*, p. 110.

[21]Eugene H. Peterson, *The Jesus Way* (Grand Rapids: Eerdmans, 2007), p. 14.

[22]Doug Pagitt, *Reimagining Spiritual Formation* (Grand Rapids: Zondervan/Emergent YS, 2003), p. 123.

[23]Graham Johnston, *Preaching to a Postmodern World* (Grand Rapids: Baker, 2001), pp. 152, 142.

[24]Kimball, *Emerging Church*, p. 179.

[25]Stanley Grenz, *Renewing the Center* (Grand Rapids: Baker, 2000), p. 317.

[26]Webber, *Ancient-Future Faith*, p. 111.

[27]C. S. Lewis, *The Inspirational Writings of C. S. Lewis*, vol. 2, *Reflections on the Psalms* (New York: Inspirational Press, 1994), p. 155.

[28]Eugene H. Peterson, *Under the Unpredictable Plant* (Grand Rapids: Eerdmans, 1992), p. 105. For method, see Eugene H. Peterson, *Answering God* (San Francisco: HarperCollins, 1989).

[29]Dietrich Bonhoeffer, *Life Together* (San Francisco: HarperCollins, 1954), p. 47.

[30]Henri J. M. Nouwen, *The Way of the Heart* (New York: Ballantine, 1981), p. 15.

[31]William Dyrness, *Visual Faith* (Grand Rapids: Baker, 2001), p. 84.

[32]Bonaventure, *The Soul's Journey into God*, Classics of Western Spirituality (Mahwah, N.J.: Paulist Press, 1978), pp. 59, 73.

[33]Eugene H. Peterson, *Eat This Book* (Grand Rapids: Eerdmans, 2006), pp. 90-117. I have found that all four movements typically associated with lectio (reading, meditation, prayer, contemplation) are a bit lengthy for a worship gathering, so we only use the first two.

[34]Ignatius of Loyola, *The Spiritual Exercises of St. Ignatius*, trans. Anthony Mattola (New York: Doubleday, 1989), pp. 54-62. For simple instructions in this form of meditation, see <www.upperroom.org/methodx/thelife/prayermethods/ignatian

.asp?iStep=1&iScriptID=>.

[35]C. S. Lewis, *The Inspirational Writings of C. S. Lewis*, vol. 1, *Surprised by Joy* (New York: Inspirational Press, 1994), p. 100.

[36]See Richard J. Foster, *Celebration of Discipline*, rev. ed. (New York: Harper & Row, 1988), pp. 30-31; and Walter Trobisch, *Martin Luther's Quiet Time* (Downers Grove, Ill.: InterVarsity Press, 1975).

[37]Ernest Southcott, quoted in Chuck Colson, *The Body* (Dallas: Word, 1992), p. 247.

Chapter 6: Communal Faith

[1]Eugene H. Peterson, *Christ Plays in Ten Thousand Places* (Grand Rapids: Eerdmans, 2005), p. 305.

[2]Ibid., p. 303.

[3]Dietrich Bonhoeffer, *Life Together* (San Francisco: HarperCollins, 1954), p. 21.

[4]Thomas Kelly, *A Testament of Devotion* (San Francisco: HarperCollins, 1941), p. 56.

[5]Gordon T. Smith, *A Holy Meal* (Grand Rapids: Baker, 2005), p. 46.

[6]Michael W. Holmes, ed., *The Apostolic Fathers* (Grand Rapids: Baker, 1989), p. 154.

[7]J. N. D. Kelly, *Early Christian Doctrines,* rev. ed. (San Francisco: Harper & Row, 1978), p. 197.

[8]Craig Blomberg, *1 Corinthians*, NIV Application Commentary (Grand Rapids: Zondervan, 1994), p. 230.

[9]Anne Lamott, quoted in Peterson, *Christ Plays in Ten Thousand Places*, p. 302.

[10]Ed Stetzer, *Planting New Churches in a Postmodern Age* (Nashville: Broadman & Holman, 2003), p. 152.

[11]Robert Webber, *The Younger Evangelicals* (Grand Rapids: Baker, 2002), p. 62.

[12]Jimmy Long, *Generating Hope* (Downers Grove, Ill.: InterVarsity Press, 1997), p. 43.

[13]Tom Beaudoin, *Virtual Faith* (San Francisco: Jossey-Bass, 1998), p. 140.

[14]Leonard Sweet, *Out of the Question . . . Into the Mystery* (Colorado Springs: Waterbrook, 2004), p. 93.

[15]Eddie Gibbs, *ChurchNext* (Downers Grove, Ill.: InterVarsity Press, 2000), p. 202.

[16]See also Joseph Myers, *Organic Community* (Grand Rapids: Baker, 2007).

[17]Joseph Myers, *The Search to Belong* (Grand Rapids: Zondervan, 2003), p. 12.

[18]Ibid., p. 39.

[19]Ibid., p. 75.

[20]Ibid., pp. 39-51.

[21]Ibid., pp. 52-54.

[22]Bonhoeffer, *Life Together*, p. 27.

[23]Ibid.

[24]Ibid., p. 28.

[25]Wade Clark Roof, *Spiritual Marketplace* (Princeton, N.J.: Princeton University Press, 1999), pp. 176-77.

[26]Eugene H. Peterson, *The Contemplative Pastor* (Grand Rapids: Eerdmans, 1993), p. 8.

[27]Tarsicius Van Bavel, *The Rule of Saint Augustine* (Kalamazoo, Mich.: Cistercian, 1996), pp. 41-52.

[28]Thomas Merton, *The Wisdom of the Desert* (New York: New Directions, 1960), p. 16.

[29]Benedict, quoted in William H. Willimon, *Pastor: The Theology and Practice of Ordained Ministry* (Nashville: Abingdon, 2002), p. 315.

[30]Timothy Fry, ed., *The Rule of Saint Benedict* (New York: Vintage, 1998), pp. 7, 55-57.

[31]George Barna, *Revolution* (Carol Stream, Ill.: Tyndale House, 2005), pp. 64-66.

[32]Todd Hunter, quoted in Eddie Gibbs and Ryan Bolger, *Emerging Churches* (Grand Rapids: Baker, 2005), p. 106. See also Eugene Peterson, *The Jesus Way* (Grand Rapids: Eerdmans, 2007), pp. 229-33.

[33]Sweet, *Out of the Question*, p. 94.

[34]Larry Crabb, *The Safest Place on Earth* (Nashville: Thomas Nelson, 1999), p. xiii.

[35]George Hunter III, *The Celtic Way of Evangelism* (Nashville: Abingdon, 2000), p. 28.

[36]Ibid., p. 21.

[37]Robert Webber, *Ancient-Future Faith* (Grand Rapids: Baker, 1999), p. 72.

[38]John Wesley, *The Works of John Wesley* (Nashville: Abingdon, 1989), 9:272-74.

[39]D. Michael Henderson, *John Wesley's Class Meeting* (Nappanee, Ind.: Francis Asbury, 1997), p. 11.

[40]Ibid., p. 131.

[41]Ibid., pp. 94, 110.

[42]For more on the format we utilize, see Neil Cole, *Organic Church* (San Francisco: Jossey-Bass, 2005), and *Cultivating a Life for God* (Carol Stream: ChurchSmart Resources, 1999).

[43]Bonhoeffer, *Life Together*, p. 110.

[44]Eugene H. Peterson, *Eat This Book* (Grand Rapids: Eerdmans, 2006), p. 61.

[45]Sweet, *Out of the Question*, p. 174.

[46]Peterson, *Christ Plays in Ten Thousand Places*, p. 206.

[47]Webber, *Ancient-Future Evangelism*, p. 58.

[48]Gibbs and Bolger, *Emerging Churches*, p. 135.

[49]Peterson, *Christ Plays in Ten Thousand Places*, p. 216.

Chapter 7: Enacted Faith

[1]Lesslie Newbigin, *The Open Secret*, rev. ed. (Grand Rapids: Eerdmans, 1995), p. 11.

[2]Gary Haugen, *Good News About Injustice* (Downers Grove, Ill.: InterVarsity Press, 1999), p. 88.

[3]See "Laundry Love Project" at <www.just4one.org/laundrylove.html>.

[4]Eugene Peterson, *Christ Plays in Ten Thousand Places* (Grand Rapids: Eerdmans, 2005), pp. 216-17.

[5]Eddie Gibbs and Ryan Bolger, *Emerging Churches* (Grand Rapids: Baker, 2005), p. 124.

[6]Erwin Raphael McManus, *An Unstoppable Force* (Loveland, Colo.: Group, 2002), p. 58.

[7]Ronald J. Sider, *Rich Christians in an Age of Hunger*, 4th ed. (Dallas: W Publishing, 1996), p. 48.

[8]Julian, quoted in Joseph H. Hellerman, *The Ancient Church as Family* (Minneapolis:

Fortress Press, 2001), pp. 224-25.

[9]Gibbs and Bolger, *Emerging Churches*, p. 128.

[10]John G. Stackhouse Jr., *Humble Apologetics* (New York: Oxford University Press, 2002), p. 135.

[11]Christopher J. H. Wright, *The Mission of God* (Downers Grove, Ill.: InterVarsity Press, 2006), p. 534.

[12]Doug Pagitt, *Reimagining Spiritual Formation* (Grand Rapids: Zondervan/Emergent YS, 2003), p. 146.

[13]Craig Detweiler and Barry Taylor, *A Matrix of Meanings* (Grand Rapids: Baker, 2003), p. 195.

[14]Philip Jenkins, *The Next Christendom* (Oxford: Oxford University Press, 2002), p. 220.

[15]Dallas Willard, *The Spirit of the Disciplines* (San Francisco: HarperCollins, 1991), p. 168.

[16]Ray S. Anderson, *An Emergent Theology for Emerging Churches* (Downers Grove, Ill.: InterVarsity Press, 2006), p. 182.

[17]Haugen, *Good News About Injustice*, p. 10.

[18]Anderson, *Emergent Theology for Emerging Churches*, p. 196.

[19]Richard Foster, *Streams of Living Water* (San Francisco: HarperCollins, 1998), pp. 136-83.

[20]David Jacobus Bosch, *Transforming Mission* (Maryknoll, N.Y.: Orbis, 1991), p. 254.

[21]Wright, *Mission of God*, pp. 317-319.

[22]Jeffrey Sachs, *The End of Poverty* (New York: Penguin, 2005), pp. 20-25.

[23]Deborah Dortzbach and W. Meredith Long, *The AIDS Crisis* (Downers Grove, Ill.: InterVarsity Press, 2006), pp. 26-27.

[24]Sachs, *End of Poverty*, p. xvi.

[25]Ibid., pp. 56-73.

[26]John Burke, *No Perfect People Allowed* (Grand Rapids: Zondervan, 2005), p. 42.